A Collector's Guide to

Chinese Dress Accessories

A Collector's Guide to

Chinese Dress Accessories

Valery M. Garrett

TIMES EDITIONS

Contents

Foreword

Imperial Chinese robes have long captured the imagination of collectors and lovers of beautiful things, for their fine embroidery and spectacular designs have a universal appeal. But these robes are rare, expensive and often difficult to display. This book turns the spotlight on the smaller accessories used from the Qing dynasty up to the middle of the twentieth century. More affordable and still quite plentiful, these accessories are often easier to display and care for.

Many works of art, including textiles, were taken out of China in times of conflict, especially during the sacking of the Summer Palace in 1860 and the Boxer Rebellion in 1900. Missionaries and traders living in China were also able to buy robes and accessories from impoverished noble families when the Qing dynasty fell in 1911. These items from time to time find their way onto the market, turning up in auction houses in the major capitals of the world and in antique shops and with private dealers. China still has a number of antique shops and street markets which are well worth exploring, for a surprising number of pieces survived the tumultuous events of the twentieth century.

In this book the use of dress accessories is first put into context with a brief overview of the styles of robes worn by the imperial Manchu rulers and their Chinese subjects. Most of these accessories were embroidered, and the methods used are discussed here. A basic introduction to Chinese symbolism is then given for a better enjoyment of the decoration on the accessories. Soft furnishings and items used in the homes of the imperial rulers as well as those of the gentry, merchants and artisans are also included. Finally there is a section on how to care for a collection.

"Quantities of embroidery are being made to meet the growing demand from abroad. Many methods, such as smoking and exposing to the sun, are resorted to to make the work appear old, but to those familiar with the older work these processes are very evident." Written in 1926,[1] these words still ring true today, now that popular accessories such as bound feet shoes are being copied. Suggestions are given on how to determine whether the piece is authentic.

My sincere thanks go to the collectors and dealers who have generously loaned items for illustration. Particular mention must go to Teresa Coleman, Judith and Ken Rutherford, Linda Wrigglesworth, Chris Hall, Eve Lee Guernier, Antonia Tozer, Don Cohn, Amanda Lack, Robert and Marilyn Hamburger and Stephen McGuinness. I am also grateful to Stephen Selby, Poh Kan Wong, James Hayes and Amy Lau, who kindly assisted in identifying some pieces. Naturally, all errors and omissions are my own.

[1] Hilda Arthurs Strong, *A Sketch of Chinese Arts and Crafts,* China Booksellers, Ltd, Peking, 1926, p. 213.

~ *Chapter One* ~

Introduction

"The walls of the Tartar City [in Beijing] heave up fifty feet in the air, and are forty feet thick. The circumference of the outer ring of fortifications is over twenty miles. Each gate is surmounted by a square three-storied tower or pagoda, vast and imposing. Round the city and through the city run century-old canals and moats with water-gates shutting down with cruel iron prongs. In the Chinese city [to the south] the two Temples of Heaven and Agriculture raise their altars to the skies, invoking the help of the deities for this decaying but proud Chinese Empire. . . . There are temples with yellow-gowned or grey-gowned priests in their hundreds founded in the times of Kublai Khan. There are Mahommedan mosques, with Chinese muezzins in blue turbans on feast days; Manchu palaces with vermilion-red pillars and archways and green and gold ceilings. There are unending lines of camels plodding slowly in from Western deserts laden with all manner of merchandise; there are curious palanquins slung between two mules and escorted by sword-armed men that have journeyed all the way from Shansi and Kansu, which are a thousand miles away; a Mongol market with bare-pated and long-coated Mongols hawking venison and other products of their chase; comely Soochow harlots with reeking native scents rising from their hair; water-carriers and barbers from sturdy Shantung; cooks from epicurean Canton; bankers from Shansi — the whole Empire of China sending its best to its old-world barbaric capital. . . .

"And right in the centre of it all is the Forbidden City, enclosing with its high pink walls the palaces which are full of warm-blooded Manchu concubines, sleek eunuchs who speak in wheedling tones, and is always hot with intrigue. At the gates of the Palace lounge bow and jingal-armed Imperial guards. Inside is the Son of Heaven himself, the Emperor imprisoned in his own Palace by the Empress Mother, who is as masterful as any man who ever lived. . . ."[1]

A colourful and poignant description of a once powerful empire, written by a resident of Beijing at the time of the Boxer Rebellion, just eleven years before the end of the feudal power of China. Crumbling and defeated, the Qing dynasty, that had begun so triumphantly, was on its knees, attacked on the outside from the west, rotten on the inside from the evil machinations of the Empress Dowager, and weakened by the neglect of a series of ineffectual emperors.

The Manchus, originally a group of semi-nomadic tribes from the northeast beyond the Great Wall, had seized power from the Chinese in 1644 and occupied the Forbidden City, which was founded by the third emperor of the Ming dynasty (1368–1644). Finding little or no resistance, they ruled over a land area of more than nine million square kilometres, covering the eighteen provinces of China and their own three provinces of Manchuria, all the way from Xinjiang in the northwest to Guangdong in the southeast. For over 250 years they held sway, until their rule was overthrown and China became a republic for the first time in its history.

Comprising only 2 per cent of a total population of some 150 million in 1700, the Manchus' immediate concern on taking control of the country was to preserve their identity and special status. Full and visible authority over the Han Chinese people was enforced by emperors who decreed that Manchu customs, language, and particularly their style of clothing should be adopted by all those connected with or in the employ of the Manchu government.

DRESS REGULATIONS

Though ultimately unsuccessful in their attempts to make the Chinese speak the Manchu language, the rulers were eager to have their style of dress worn by all those who were eligible. To do this, Regulations first set down in 1636, before the conquest, were revised and extended in 1644. By 1759, the Qianlong Emperor (ruled 1736–1795) was sufficiently concerned that Manchu costume was being diluted by Chinese style that he commissioned "The Illustrated Precedents for the Ritual Paraphernalia of the Imperial Court" (*Huangchao liqi tushi*), which was published and enforced in 1766. [2]

The eighteen chapters of the *Huangchao liqi tushi* set down rules on such topics as ritual vessels, astronomical instruments, musical instruments, military uniforms, and especially the dress of the Manchu imperial family of emperors, princes, noblemen and their consorts, as well as Manchu officials and their wives. Among the Han Chinese, it included those men who had passed the difficult civil service examinations and attained the rank of mandarin, the scholar officials who carried out the emperor's commands.[3] This system of dress Regulations served to help unite the country and made the dress of the Han Chinese officials indistinguishable from their Manchu rulers.

There were rules governing the changing of clothing according to season, the timing of which was dictated by the Official Gazette from Beijing. This stated the month, day and hour that the emperor would change his clothing for the season. At this time all those wearing official dress were required to do likewise. Anyone found not wearing the correct attire and headwear was subjected to severe punishment. However, the rules did not just apply to the officials but to the lower orders, too. "The requirements of etiquette were most exacting, when one realises that a complete change of costume was called for, not only for the four seasons, . . . but very often for the twenty-four fortnightly periods of the Chinese calendar. . . . For those who followed the fashion, by choice or obligation, each season demanded the most rigid observation."[4]

Despite the insistence that rules be followed, there appears to have been some borrowing of styles by both Manchu and Chinese. The practise

[PLATE 1] Left: The Qianlong Emperor wearing official formal court dress for summer.
[PLATE 2] Right: Empress Xiaoxian, wife of the Qianlong Emperor, wearing full winter court attire.

was apparently sufficiently widespread that the Daoguang Emperor (ruled 1821–1850) found it necessary to issue a decree complaining that, despite existing laws, Manchus were wearing Chinese dress. The borrowing was particularly prevalent later in the dynasty, when traditions had loosened, between Manchu women and Han Chinese women, the latter having no role in the Manchu government and their dress not being covered by the Regulations. Photographs taken in Beijing and Hong Kong at the end of the nineteenth century show that these cross-cultural adaptations must have been very tempting, especially to fashionable women, as an opportunity to wear different styles of dress.[5]

Official Dress

As ordained by the Regulations, clothing was divided into official and non-official, then sub-divided according to the degree of formality. Official formal court robes and semi-formal robes were decorated with dragons to indicate rank, and worn when attending to matters of state. Accessories were an important element of the court dress shown in the Regulations. Those worn by the emperor, princes, noblemen and officials included hats and hat finials, collars, girdles, and neck chains. For female members of the imperial household, accessories included headwear and several items of jewellery.

A portrait of the Qianlong Emperor in **Plate 1** shows him wearing official formal dress for summer: court robe, court hat, girdle with purses attached, court chain, collar and boots. In **Plate 2**, Empress Xiaoxian (1712–1748), the young wife of the Qianlong Emperor, is shown wearing the full winter court attire of robe and collar trimmed with black fur, overvest, hat, diadem, torque necklace, *zai shui* pendant and three court chains. Court dress for officials is pictured in **Figure 1**, where a Chinese mandarin wears a robe partially covered by a surcoat bearing an insignia badge denoting rank, together with a summer hat, collar, neck chain and boots.

Although, as already mentioned, Han Chinese women were not required to follow the Regulations, when appearing on important occasions in the company of their high-ranking husbands they wore quasi-official garments which had developed from those worn by noblewomen during the Chinese-governed Ming dynasty. In this way they were able to show respect and loyalty to their ancestors. The stole, or *xia pei,* seen here in **Figure 1** worn by the mandarin's wife, is decorated with dragons, and has insignia squares on the back and chest which correspond in rank to that of her husband. It is worn over a hip-length jacket decorated with more dragons and a finely pleated skirt with panels back and front from under which her tiny bound feet shoes are visible. An elaborate coronet and neck chain complete the outfit.

For non-official occasions Chinese men and women were free to wear their own style of dress. In this group photo taken circa 1905 (**Figure 2**) the women are wearing bulky hip length jackets with wide contrasting bands of colour and long sleeves covering the hands. The two standing women are wearing trousers, which suggests they are unmarried. The men also wear robes with

[FIG 1] A Cantonese mandarin and his wife in their official robes, circa 1860.

[FIG 2] A group of Han Chinese men and women wearing informal dress, circa 1905.

long sleeves, as it was considered impolite to show the hands. Waistcoats complete their informal attire.[6]

DECORATION

Clothing and accessories were often highly decorated with auspicious symbols designed to protect the wearer or to invoke favourable responses from the gods. Members of the imperial family, officials and their wives would have presented a very colourful appearance indeed.

The five colours favoured by the Ming rulers continued to have symbolic properties for the Manchus. Yellow stood for the centre and the earth. It was reserved for the emperor and his consorts. Blue represented spring and the east. Because the Manchus adopted blue as their dynastic colour, the court and dragon robes worn by mandarins were blue. Green was considered to be a shade of blue.[7] Red symbolised summer and the south, but this colour was generally avoided as it had been the dynastic colour of the Ming. However, because of the connection with the Ming rulers, it was considered a lucky colour by the Han Chinese and used extensively for weddings and celebrations. White represented autumn and the west, but as it was associated with death it was felt to be an unlucky colour to wear. Black stood for winter and the north.

Before the invention in England in 1856 of aniline dyes and their introduction into China around 1870, all dyes were produced from plants. These vegetable dyes were made by combining plants with water and a mordant, or fixing agent. Today many collectors of textiles and embroidery prefer the more mellow tones of the vegetable dyes to the strident shades of the aniline dyes, but one can imagine and understand the excitement caused by the vivid pinks, lime greens and turquoises when they first became available. A rough guide to dating can be based on the type of dye used.

Embroidery

Embroidery in China has a long history dating back to the invention of silk four thousand years ago. Within the Qing dynasty, the designs and applied decoration reached a peak during the relatively stable and peaceful reigns of the Kangxi (ruled 1662–1722), Yongzheng (ruled 1723–1735) and Qianlong Emperors. Embroidery became an industry in itself, with men, women and children engaged in its manufacture. A lady in a well-to-do household, untutored in formal education and often illiterate, would learn to do exquisite embroidery as a feminine accomplishment. In this way she could prove her skills to her prospective husband and mother-in-law. Many households also employed an embroiderer to produce the many articles they required. Embroidery studios flourished in order to keep pace with demand.

The base cloth for embroidery was usually silk, of every weight from gauze to satin, although cotton was also used in a small way. Men worked standing at an embroidery frame made of bamboo suspended from the wall, with the material to be worked on stretched tightly across it. Women worked sitting down with the frame supported by their legs, as their bound feet prevented them from standing for any length of time. Children sat at a high table frame.

Books of woodcuts printed on rice paper, showing the approved styles of embroidery and the arrangement of colours and patterns, were a popular reference for embroidery designs. Some were designed to be scaled up for large hangings or garments. Small designs were copied directly onto the cloth by pricking around the outline and dusting white powder through the holes. Coloured rice paper cuts, made to be pasted onto the paper windows found in many Chinese homes, were also used as a base for design on small articles. Stencils were made of the most popular designs and symbols, and many large embroidery studios had a selection of cardboard templates which were used to give uniformity, to assist in placing the design, and to save time.

Very short (about 3-centimetre), fine needles were used, initially made of ivory or bone, later of copper, bronze or steel. Silks for embroidery were bought from itinerant peddlers who walked the streets twirling a rattle to announce their wares. They carried small drawers of floss and twisted silk in every shade imaginable, as well as silver- and gold-covered thread.

Stitches

Although there was not a great number of different stitches, often a stitch had many variations and went by a variety of names. Most are familiar to embroiderers in the west, such as buttonhole stitch, chain stitch, cross stitch, and counted, or tent, stitch. Satin stitch was used extensively. The stitches had to be very flat and even to give the characteristic satin-smooth appearance. Voiding—leaving a hair's breadth of fabric between adjacent areas of satin stitch to give definition to the design—was favoured, especially in Shanghai, in the early years of the twentieth century. Other variations of satin stitch were brick stitch and bargello, which give interesting textured effects. Long-and-short stitch is made by making the first row of stitches alternately long and short; thereafter all the rows have stitches the same length. It was used to give gradations of colour and shade.

Couching was popular as a way to anchor gold and silver threads, which could not be sewn directly as they might split the silk cloth. The threads were laid in rows on the surface of the cloth, and a toning silk thread was employed to anchor them in position. Towards the end of the nineteenth century red and green silk was used for couching, as these colours were thought to enhance the metal thread.

Bales of peacock feathers, sent as tribute from Annam and other countries in the south during the Ming dynasty, had been found by the Manchus in storehouses in the Forbidden City.[8] These feathers were also couched and used, especially at the beginning of the Qing dynasty, when there was a severe shortage of silk from the silk-producing regions in the south, caused by the Manchu invasion.

Two stitches which were particularly Chinese in origin were Pekinese stitch and Peking knot. Pekinese stitch is formed when a backstitch is interlaced with a looped second thread, giving a neat textured effect. Seed stitch, *da zi* in Chinese (meaning 'making seeds', a reference to the smallness and evenness of the stitch), was better known as Peking knot. The stitch was used to give a soft texture, to fill in small areas, or to define details. It has been called 'blind stitch' by some westerners because it was said to ruin the eyesight of the embroiderers, and also 'forbidden stitch' for the same reason, although there is no legal evidence of such a ban. In fact, several other stitches are equally small and intricate, so the term may relate to the fact it was associated with those living in the Forbidden City.

Other Methods of Decoration

In addition to embroidery, there were also other forms of decoration. A type of woven silk tapestry, particularly refined by the Chinese, was known as *kesi*. Literally meaning 'cut silk', each colour doubled back on itself, without any floating threads across the back. It was linked to the next colour at the corners, causing tiny slits to be visible between each colour. These slits make the fabric fragile, and consequently *kesi* pieces are quite scarce. Appliquéd silk or cotton motifs were also used, and some beadwork was done using tiny Peking glass beads sewn in floral designs, particularly on headbands and shoe vamps.

By the first quarter of the twentieth century applied decoration had lost favour, as new weaves and improved printing methods made unadorned fabrics more popular. Emancipation for women and dramatic changes in the social order meant that women had less time for painstaking handwork. Today, apart from traditional Chinese wedding garments and household linens and embroidered panels made for tourists and produced in embroidery studios, only the minority groups of non Han Chinese people living in remote areas continue the tradition of decorating clothing for their own use.

Endnotes

[1] B.L.Putnam Weale, *Indiscreet Letters from Peking*, Hurst and Blackett, Ltd., London, 1900, pp. 27–28.

[2] One set of paintings on silk, thought to be part of the Regulations removed from the Yuanmingyuan (the Summer Palace on the outskirts of Beijing), survives in the Victoria & Albert Museum in London. Bound volumes of the Regulations using woodblock prints on paper were also in circulation so that those concerned could refer to them freely.

[3] For more information on the role, duties and dress of the mandarin, see Valery M. Garrett, *Mandarin Squares: Mandarins and their Insignia,* OUP, Hong Kong, 1990.

[4] Hilda Arthurs Strong, *A Sketch of Chinese Arts and Crafts,* China Booksellers, Ltd, Peking, 1926, p. 207.

[5] A. C. Scott, *Chinese Costume In Transition*, Donald Moore, Singapore, 1958, p. 47.

[6] Manchu court robes and Han Chinese dress in particular are covered in more detail in Valery M. Garrett, *Chinese Clothing: An Illustrated Guide*, OUP, Hong Kong, 1994.

[7] The cloth was first dyed yellow, then re-dyed with indigo blue to make green. However, as the yellow dye was fugitive, after awhile the appearance was more blue than green.

[8] Schuyler Cammann, *Chinese Mandarin Squares: Brief Catalogue of the Letcher Collection*, The University Museum Bulletin, University of Pennsylvania, June 1953, p. 12.

~ *Chapter Two* ~

Chinese Symbolism

Symbolism plays an important role in the folklore of most societies, with certain objects or species being endowed with protective or propitious properties. The superstitious Chinese placed great faith in supernatural powers. Symbolism was employed in three ways: to invoke good fortune, to outwit the evil forces ever present and to imply status. Very often combinations of these types were used together.

Good fortune was naturally desired by all and was epitomised by symbols for long life, abundance and happiness. The latter half of the nineteenth century was a time of uncertainty in China, and many propitious symbols were used to summon favourable spiritual powers. Dragon robes and insignia badges particularly gained many emblems dispersed across the background. Sleevebands which edged the cuffs on the hip-length jackets worn by Han Chinese women were also popular places for symbols of good fortune.

Children were particularly at risk as, before basic hygiene improved and medical care was more widespread, many infants died before their first birthday. This was always seen as a result of evil spirits in the air all around waiting to whisk the child away. Thus the natural desire of parents was to combat these evil forces in nature. It was unthinkable for a mother to send her child out into the world unprotected. Clothing and accessories were covered with auspicious symbols and pictures of fierce animals to consume the offending spirits.

Becoming a wealthy and influential official was largely dependent on passing examinations founded on a thorough knowledge of the Chinese classics. Subjects such as science, foreign languages and mathematics were dismissed as irrelevant. This preoccupation with literary ability led to subtle puns based on the phonetic tones of the Chinese language. Representations of abstract concepts by pictures or symbols were used by many scholars and indicated a high level of literary taste. For instance, a lotus flower with an egret symbolises the honesty of an uncorrupt official, as the bird keeps its white plumage clean even in the dirty water of a lotus pond. Another symbol frequently portrayed was that of a deer holding a sacred fungus in its mouth, as it was said that the deer was the only animal able to find this plant of long life. Even to the uneducated many natural species, such as flowers, insects, birds and animals, were considered auspicious because the homonym sounded the same as something thought to be lucky.

Finally, in a country where the majority of the population was illiterate, pictorial proof of rank, as well as literary scholarship, visibly

showed superior status. For example, the number of dragons and the number of their claws were ordained by the Regulations to denote rank. Nine dragons were stipulated for the semi-formal robes of an emperor, while eight or five were worn by lowlier officials. A five-clawed dragon, *long*, was the preserve of the emperor, unless he had accorded its use to a deserving subordinate, and this had superior status over a four-clawed dragon, *mang*, worn by lesser noblemen and officials. At first these rules were strictly regulated, but by the end of the Qing dynasty, when traditional laws began to be more freely interpreted, even wealthy merchants began buying degrees and then ranks and took to wearing robes bearing nine dragons with five claws.[1] This was only one of many ways of indicating social position. Those expressed by the wearing of different accessories are covered later in the book.

AUSPICIOUS MOTIFS

Listed below are some of the most common patterns and motifs which have been endowed by the Chinese with symbolic meaning.

BAMBOO This stands for longevity and courage in adversity, as it is an evergreen. Because it grows straight it is a popular symbol for mandarins and represents an honest official.

BATS The homonym *fu* stands for both 'bat' and 'happiness', hence the bat is a popular symbol. Five bats shown together signify the Five Blessings: longevity, health, wealth, virtue, and a natural death. Shown here in **Plate 1** is a sleeveband from a woman's jacket showing the bat with a peony embroidered in Peking knot. The combination of three shades of blue (light, medium and dark), called *san laan*, was used extensively on clothing worn by married women, particularly at the time of marriage, as this was the first occasion she was entitled to wear this combination.

BUDDHA'S HAND The name given to a citrus fruit, as it resembles a hand with fingers outstretched to grasp money. It symbolises wealth and divine protection and is shown in **Plate 2** on a child's collar which has been embroidered in voided satin stitch.

BUTTERFLY An old and very common symbol that suggests the meaning 'great age' because in Chinese *die* also sounds like the word for seventy or eighty years of age. It is also a symbol of joy and marital happiness. Shown in **Plate 3** is a butterfly on a sleeveband which is embroidered in satin stitch in aniline dyes.

CATS They have the ability to see in the dark, hence they can spot evil lurking. They were known as protectors of silk worms because they catch the rats which eat the worms. The word for cat, *mao*, and for octogenarian are similar, so the cat is a wish for longevity.

CHRYSANTHEMUM One of four important flower emblems signifying autumn and a contented middle age.

CICADA Represents eternal youth and immortality.

[PLATE 1]
Opposite, top: Bat and peony embroidered in Peking knot in the 'three blues' on a ladies' sleeveband, mid-nineteenth century. Collection of the author.

[PLATE 2]
Above: Child's collar showing the golden 'Buddha's hand' citrus fruit on the left, embroidered in voided satin stitch, late nineteenth century. Collection of the author.

[PLATE 3]
Opposite, bottom: Butterfly embroidered on a sleeveband in satin stitch using aniline dyes, late nineteenth century. Collection of the author.

CLOUDS Stylised clouds were a symbol of heaven and fertility. They were useful as space fillers and to unify a design.

COCKEREL Heralds the dawn, and its crowing represents achievement and fame; it is the emblem of an official.

COINS A symbol of the desire for wealth.

CRANE The crane is another longevity symbol, as the bird is said to live for two thousand years. A bird flying or looking towards the sun represents a desire to rise high in the government hierarchy.

CRICKET This is a symbol of courage and of summer.

DEER The homonym *lu* also means an official's salary, hence it is a sign of wealth and achievement. Shown in **Plate 4** is a pair of sleevebands containing a deer with *lingzhi,* or sacred fungus, the crane and the cypress tree, all embroidered in couched gold and silver thread. These are all symbols of longevity and immortality.

DRAGON The dragon is a benevolent creature and the emblem of imperial authority. It is also used in connection with marriage, as it is a symbol of male vigour and fertility, as well symbolising the emperor when it represents the bridegroom on his wedding day. Shown in **Plate 5** is a pair of gold and silver couched sleevebands from a Chinese lady's wedding jacket. The writhing dragon is shown above a *li shui* hem against a background of *shou* characters, while flying down towards it is a phoenix, symbol of the bride.

FISH A homonym for fish, *yu*, means superfluity. Because fish are seldom seen alone, the fish is an emblem of wealth and abundance. Owing to its reproductive powers, it is also the symbol of regeneration, and because it is happy in its natural habitat it symbolises harmony and happiness. The dragon fish represents a carp changing into a dragon and is a symbol for the successful passing of an examination. The beautiful pair of sleevebands in **Plate 6** show goldfish swimming amid peonies.

FLAMES Stylised flames often surround mythical and mystical emblems. They are used also to symbolise fire and consuming energy.

HORSE This is an emblem of speed and perseverance. Only high officials were allowed to ride on a horse, hence it is also seen as a wish for high office.

HUNDRED BOYS This shows a wish for many sons. Those seen in **Plate 7** are embroidered in satin stitch on a pair of sleevebands. They are often put on bed hangings to encourage fertility.

LI SHUI *Li shui,* meaning 'upright water', is the name for the diagonal bands at the base of the dragon robes and the lower part of insignia squares; they are repeated here at the base of the sleevebands in **Plate 5**.

LION This is a fierce animal which protects children from harm; it is often depicted in green.

LOTUS The lotus is an emblem of purity, fruitfulness and perfection. One of the four important flower emblems, it symbolises summer. It is also an important motif in Chinese art, where it represents the Buddha. It is the emblem of redemption and purity because it grows out of mud but its blossom is undefiled.

[PLATE 4]

Opposite: Deer on a pair of uncut sleevebands, together with the sacred fungus, crane and cypress tree, all symbols of longevity, embroidered in couched gold and silver thread, late nineteenth century. Collection of the author.

[PLATE 5] Left: Dragon and phoenix on a pair of sleevebands from a lady's wedding jacket, mid-nineteenth century. Collection of the author.
[PLATE 6] Right: Goldfish with peonies are combined on this exquisite pair of sleevebands, early nineteenth century. Collection of the author.
[PLATE 7] Opposite: Hundred Boys are embroidered here in satin stitch on a beautiful pair of sleevebands, mid-nineteenth century. Collection of the author.

Shown in **Plate 8** is a sleeveband showing a lotus flower with fish swimming. The silk has been appliquéd and then painted in delicate shades.

MAGNOLIA BLOSSOM A symbol of female beauty.

MANDARIN DUCK These are always shown in pairs representing male and female, and stand for marital fidelity and happiness. If separated, the birds pine away and die. It is often pictured with beautiful plumage, as seen in **Plate 9** on a section of a pillowcase made for a wedding bed.

MOUNTAINS A symbol of earth, steadfastness and longevity. They are one of the elements of the cosmos, together with *li shui*

NARCISSUS A sign of winter and of the Lunar New Year.

PEACH The blossom is a symbol of springtime, marriage and immortality. The fruit is a symbol of longevity and said to be the food of life, especially of the Eight Immortals. Shown on a sleeveband in **Plate 10** are peaches with cranes amid flowers, edged with the Buddhist Endless Knot and all embroidered in satin stitch.

PEONY Another of the four flower emblems, the peony signifyies summer, love and affection. It also indicates a hope for greater advancement and is shown in **Plates 1 and 6**.

PHOENIX An ancient emblem signifying goodness and benevolence. It was used to symbolise the Empress of China and, on her wedding day, the bride. It is shown in **Plate 5** with a dragon. The phoenix is also a symbol of high achievement, as this bird can fly the closest to heaven.

PINE One of the ten longevity symbols; because it is an evergreen it stands for long life, vigour, strength and vitality.

[PLATE 8]
Opposite, left: Lotus flower with fish on a sleeveband which is appliquéd and painted on silk, late nineteenth century. Collection of the author.

[PLATE 9]
Above: Pair of mandarin ducks embroidered in aniline dyes on a pillowcase for a wedding bed, circa 1930. Collection of the author.

[PLATE 10]
Opposite, right: The peach, the crane and the Endless Knot are combined on a late nineteenth century sleeveband. Collection of the author.

PLUM BLOSSOM The plum blossom, or prunus, is the last of the four flower emblems. It symbolises winter and long life because the blossom appears on leafless branches. The delicate pink flowers with their five petals also epitomise beauty.

POMEGRANATE With its many seeds, the pomegranate symbolises abundance and a desire for many sons.

QILIN A mythical composite beast with a dragon's head, a scaly body, a bushy lion's tail, a pair of horns and horse's hooves. It represents high rank and is thought to have great wisdom.

RUYI This is a sceptre and a symbol of rank, standing for 'as you wish', or 'all you desire'.

SACRED FUNGUS The *lingzhi* represents eternal life and is one of the ten symbols of

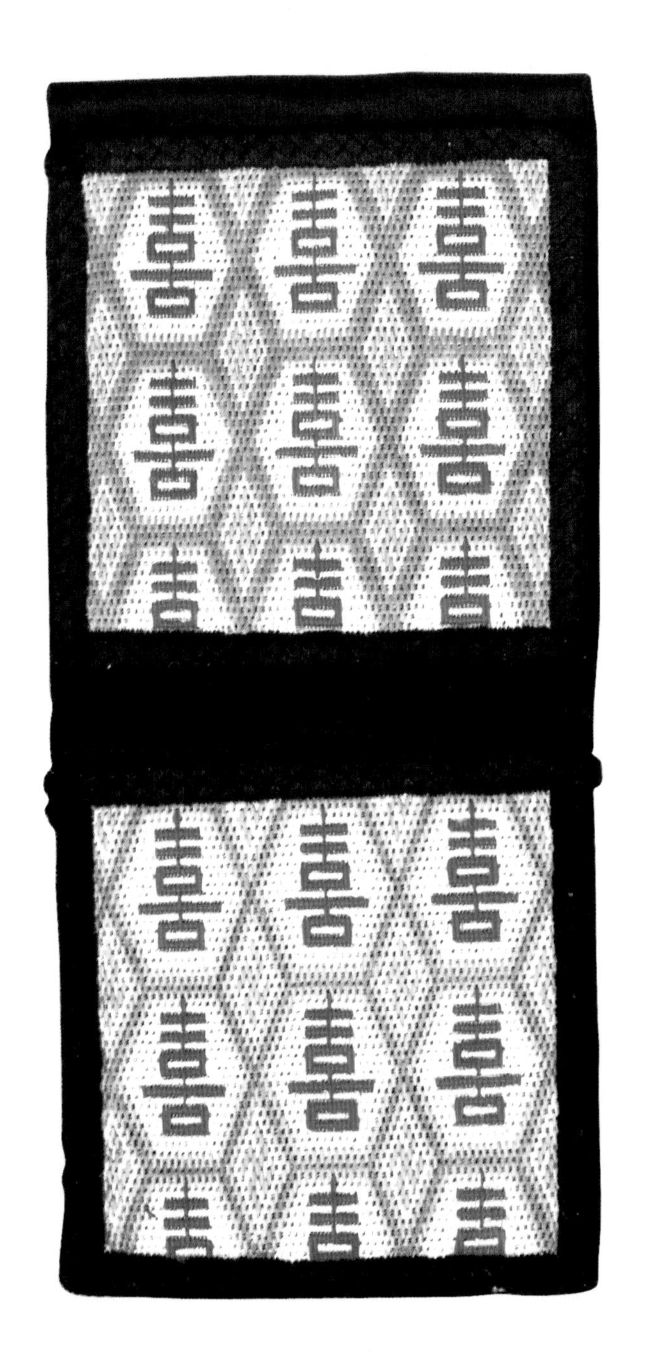

longevity. It is often depicted as an amorphous shape with holes and striped in shades of blue. One rendering is shown below in **Plate 13**.

SHOU The character for long life can, it is said, be depicted in up to a hundred different variations. When combined with the bat it stands for long life and happiness. The *shou* character is shown in two variations embroidered in Pekinese stitch in the centre of the three purses in **Plate 11**.

SHUANGXI Meaning 'double happiness', *shuangxi* is depicted by the character *xi* ('happiness') repeated twice; as such it is always associated with marriage. It is shown in **Plate 11**. The single character is on the purse on the left, while the one on the right has the double character, both embroidered in brick stitch. Other characters on the righthand purse are for good fortune and long life.

SUN A symbol of heaven and the emperor, and of intellectual enlightenment.

THUNDER LINE Another prehistoric emblem dating from the Shang dynasty or before, its name comes from its resemblance to the ancient Chinese character for thunder. Often used as a border design, it is sometimes combined with the *wan* motif.

TIGER The king of beasts, a fierce animal which protects children from evil.

VASE Stands for peace because the Chinese word *ping* is a homonym for peace; it is one of the Hundred Treasures, symbols of antiquity.

WAN One of the oldest design symbols in the world, said to have been associated with prehistoric shaman rituals. Often confused with the

[PLATE 11]
Opposite: Double Happiness, *wan*, and *shou* characters are shown on these three purses; circa 1870. Collection of the author.

swastika, it is taken to mean 'ten thousand years of long life'. It is seen embroidered in yellow on the purse on the far left and right of **Plate 11**.

YIN YANG A symbol of the interaction of opposites in nature. The light portion, *yang*, signifies the male and odd numbers, while the dark side, *yin*, symbolizes the female and even numbers (**Figure 1**).

Many symbols were grouped together, either in sets of three or five, or most commonly in sets of eight, all considered to be lucky numbers.

THREE FRIENDS IN WINTER The cypress, pine and bamboo: these evergreens, which do not wither in winter, represent friends who remain constant in adversity.

THREE LUCKY FRUITS These are the peach, pomegranate and Buddha's hand.

FOUR NOBLE FLOWERS Also called Flowers of the Four Seasons: plum blossom for winter, magnolia or orchid for spring; peony or lotus for summer; and chrysanthemum for autumn.

THE FOUR ATTRIBUTES OF THE SCHOLAR These are books, scroll paintings, lute and chess-board. They were popular in the nineteenth century, as they represented to the beleaguered officials the leisurely life of contemplation which they hoped was to follow in retirement. The scroll paintings and books are seen on a framed purse in **Plate 12**.

FIVE POISONS Also called the Five Evil Creatures: the snake, three-legged toad, scorpion, spider and centipede. They are often shown together on children's clothing as a talisman to ward off evil. Shown in **Plate 13** is a roundel with a winged tiger standing over the sacred fungus from which a snake is appearing. The tiger is surrounded by the scorpion, a monkey holding a spider, the centipede and a strange-looking four-legged toad!

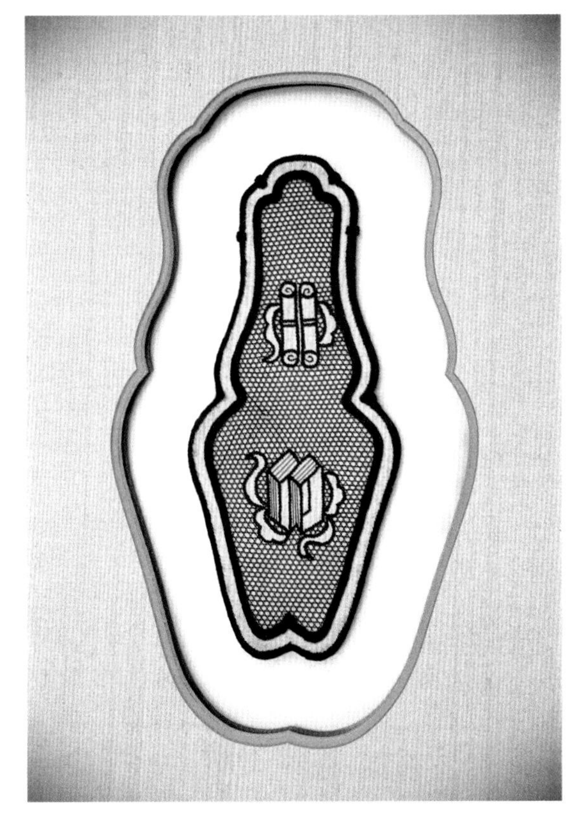

[PLATE 12]
Left: Two of the Four Attributes of the Scholar are shown on this gourd-shaped purse, mid-nineteenth century. Collection of the author.

Plate 13)
Opposite: Five Poisons surround the winged tiger; circa 1900. Collection of the author.

[FIG 1]
Below: The yin yang symbol with the Eight Trigrams displayed around it.

EIGHT TRIGRAMS Also called *Ba Gua*, this was the basis of an ancient system of divination and philosophy. It is a mystical symbol showing eight groups of triple broken and unbroken lines representing the eight points of the compass. These are arranged in a circle with the *yin yang* symbol in the centre, as shown in **Figure 1**. It was used as a talisman against evil.

TEN LONGEVITY SYMBOLS These are

the bamboo, the butterfly, clouds, mountains, the peach, the pine, the plum blossom, the sacred fungus, *shou* and *wan*.

TWELVE ANIMALS OF THE ZODIAC These are the rat, ox, tiger, hare, dragon, snake, horse, goat, monkey, cockerel, dog and pig. The year 1997, for instance, is the Year of the Ox.

In addition, many supernatural powers were called upon, several of which are illustrated in the following chapters. The most popular were:

FU LU SHOU The three mythological figures denoting good fortune, an abundance of good things, and long life respectively.

HE HE The Heavenly Twins—these two little boys are symbols of peace and harmony!

SHOU XING The God of Longevity.

THE EIGHT DAOIST IMMORTALS Each Immortal represents a different condition in life: poverty, wealth, aristocracy, plebianism, youth, age, masculinity and femininity. All are said to have drunk the Elixir of Life and become indestructible. They are a popular inspiration to artists and poets, and their individual legends are well known in Chinese folklore.

Zhongli Quan, the chief of the Immortals and patron saint of the military, is always portrayed as a fat man with a bare stomach and carrying a fan and a peach. Lu Dongbin is portrayed with a sword at his back, a scholar warrior and patron of the literati. Li Tiegui, often known as Iron Crutch Li, is portrayed as a beggar with an iron crutch and a gourd. He is the patron saint of the sick. Cao Guojin wears court dress and holds castanets. He represents officialdom, and is the patron saint of actors (**Plate 14**). Han Xiangci personifies youth and is usually shown holding a flute as the patron of musicians, while Lan Caihe carries a flower basket and is the patron saint of gardeners. Zhang Guolao carries a bamboo tube and two sticks. He is the patron saint of artists and calligraphers, seen in **Plate 15**. Last is He Xiangu, the only woman, who carries a lotus and is patron saint of housewives.

THE EIGHT DAOIST EMBLEMS These are all symbols of the Daoist patron saints and are carried by the Eight Immortals. They are seen in **Figure 2**.

Fan - symbol of Zhongli Quan, patron saint of the military.

Sword - symbol of Lu Dongbin, a scholar-warrior and patron of barbers.

Gourd - with the crutch, the symbol of Li Tiegui, the patron saint of the sick.

Castanets - symbol of Cao Guojin, patron saint of actors.

Flute - symbol of Han Xiangci, patron saint of musicians.

Flower basket - symbol of Lan Caihe, patron saint of gardeners and florists.

Bamboo tube and rods - symbol of Zhang Guolao, patron saint of artists and calligraphers.

Lotus - symbol of He Xiangu, patron saint of housewives.

[PLATE 14] Left: One of the Eight Immortals, Cao Guojin, on a birthday hanging, 1927. Collection of the author.
[PLATE 15] Right: Another of the Eight Immortals, Zhang Guolao, on a birthday hanging, dated 1927. Collection of the author.

[FIG 2] The emblems of the Eight Immortals.

[FIG 3] The Eight Treasures.

[FIG 4)] The Eight Buddhist Emblems.

THE EIGHT PRECIOUS THINGS These are also known as the Eight Treasures and are shown in **Figure 3**.

Pearl - good fortune
Coin - wealth
Lozenge - victory
Mirror - conjugal happiness
Stone Chime - happiness
Books - wisdom
Rhinoceros horn cups - health
Artemesia leaf - happiness

THE EIGHT BUDDHIST EMBLEMS These are seen here in **Figure 4**.

Wheel of the Law - symbol of Buddhist teaching, which leads the disciple to nirvana.

Conch shell - originally used to call the faithful to prayer, this is a Buddhist symbol of victory.

Umbrella - a symbol of nobility which sheds the heat of desire.

Canopy - a symbol of victory over the religions of the world.

Lotus - symbol of purity and the promise of nirvana.

Jar - called the 'treasury of all desires' and said to contain the elixir of heaven.

Pair of fish - happiness and the symbol of *yin* and *yang*, the female (*yin*) and male (*yang*) principles. Signifies a balance of opposites in nature.

Endless Knot - symbolises the Buddhist path and the 'thread' which guides one to happiness; it is seen in **Plate 10**.

Endnote

[1] It had been possible from the start of the Qing dynasty to purchase an academic degree and then an official rank and title, but this process increased towards the end of the dynasty.

[PLATE 3]
Mandarin's winter hat with sealskin brim and crystal hat button; mandarin's summer hat with fine silk fringing and coral hat button; hat stands of blue and white ceramic and wood inlaid with mother of pearl; stacking hat box for winter and summer hat, nineteenth century. Collection of the author. Ivory hat stand, early nineteenth century. Jobrenco Ltd, Chris Hall Collection Trust.

~ *Chapter Three* ~

Headwear

A hat was the most visible accessory and, as a significant part of official dress, was worn on every public occasion. The importance of headwear for both men and women is shown by the fact that hats come first in each set of Regulations for court dress illustrated in the *Huangchao liqi tushi*. The insignia on the hat was the most notable part of the headwear and is discussed in greater detail in Chapter 4.

MEN'S HEADWEAR

Court Hat

Official hats were subdivided according to season and worn with the requisite official robes. Summer hats were worn from the third month of the lunar calendar until the eighth month, when they were replaced by winter hats. With formal court attire the emperor, princes, noblemen and high officials wore a court hat known as a *chao guan*. For winter, this hat had a turned-up brim of sable or fox fur and a padded crown covered in red floss silk teased at the edges to stand out. The one shown in **Plate 1** belonged to a high-ranking official; on merit, he had been awarded by the emperor the right to wear the attached peacock plume.

For summer the hat was cone-shaped to shade the face from the sun. It was made of finely woven split bamboo covered with silk gauze edged with a narrow band of brocade, with a circle of brocade at the apex for the hat finial to rest on. A fringe of red floss silk covered the crown from apex to edge. The *chao guan* in **Plate 2** belonged to the Qianlong Emperor.

Ji Guan

A *ji guan*, or festive hat, was worn on semi-formal occasions with the dragon robe, or *ji fu*. During the designated winter months, officials in the Manchu government wore the *ji guan* with a turned-up brim of black satin, velvet, sealskin or mink. The black silk quilted crown was covered with red silk fringing. In the centre front of **Plate 3** the winter hat has a sealskin brim, quilted black satin crown and thick red twisted silk fringing. It is lined with red silk and topped with a crystal hat button, indicating the wearer was a fifth rank official.

For summer, the conical hat was made of split bamboo covered with silk gauze for high officials, as seen in **Plate 3**. It has fine red silk fringing from the apex to the edge of the brim, and the coral hat button with the *shou* character at the front indicates the wearer was an official of the second rank. The hat is lined with red silk with a stiffened sweatband of woven rattan covered in red cotton, with strings attached to tie under the chin. When first introduced, in

[PLATE 1]
Above: High-ranking official's winter *chao guan* with 'double-eyed' peacock feather plume and hat finial. Courtesy of Murray Warner Collection of Oriental Art, University of Oregon Museum of Art.

[PLATE 2]
Below: Qianlong Emperor's summer *chao guan* with gold and pearl finial. National Palace Museum, Taipei.

[FIG 1]
Crow feather plume in a flat wooden box; double-eyed peacock feather plume; lacquered case for the plume, 1876. Collection of the author.

1646, an official noted that a shortage in southern China meant they had to be cut out of baskets and straw mats.[1] Those made for use by high officials were supplied by villagers around Chengdu in Sichuan Province. The hats took two days or more to weave, and the skill was passed down from generation to generation.

Military men and guards had red horse hair or yak hair instead of the silk fringing on summer hats. This extended beyond the brim to keep flies out of the eyes while on sentry duty. Lower-ranking public servants, including attendants in processions, insignia bearers and clerks to officials, wore the summer hat made of woven straw with red fringing; their winter hat had a brim of black satin or cotton.

Hat Stands and Hat Boxes

When at home, the mandarin would remove his hat and place it on a stand. Some stands were cylindrical and made of ceramic or bamboo with apertures to ventilate the hat, while others were collapsible and could easily be transported when the mandarin went on a tour of his district. In **Plate 3** the summer hat is placed on a blue and white ceramic stand. Beside it is a collapsible wooden stand which slides apart, lacquered and inlaid with mother of pearl. The other collapsible stand on the left is made of carved and pierced ivory, and dates to the early nineteenth century.

Hat boxes were designed to hold a single winter or summer hat and were made of lacquered leather or covered with blue cotton or silk. Some boxes had an inside compartment in the centre of the base with a lid, which was a convenient place to store the neck chain worn by the mandarin. Stacking pairs of hat boxes that held the winter hat in the base and the summer hat above were carried by the official's attendant if the mandarin knew he would be away from home when the edict was issued to change from summer attire to winter attire or vice versa. **Plate 3** shows a stacking hat box made of lacquered leather, the label inside stating it was made by 'Fung Yuen Shing, manufacturers of leather cases, hat boxes and pillows' in Guangzhou.

Feather Plumes

Officials were graded from first rank down to ninth rank. As a sign of great honour, peacock feather plumes, *hua yu,* could be awarded to officials of the fifth rank and above by the emperor for exemplary services rendered. The feather plume would be attached through a small tube to the apex of the hat next to the hat finial. One, two or three overlapping peacock feathers were worn: the more eyes, the greater the honour. However, towards the end of the dynasty these were openly for sale, with one example in the Victoria & Albert Museum in London still bearing a label from the Wan Sheng Yong Feather Shop in the main street in Beijing.[2]

Tubes of yellow silk-covered paper were used to protect the peacock feathers, which were then encased in a rigid box. Seen here in **Figure 1** on the right is a peacock plume next to a lacquered, cylindrical plume holder, the inscription on it reading 'the merit of a good officer: yield when

[PLATE 4]
Opposite: Long horsehair plume dyed red and short silk fringing in boxes. Black horsehair plume in a blue box, for a military officer. Collection of the author.

[FIG 2]
Right: Emperor's informal skull cap in dark blue satin, appliquéd and topped with a red silk knot and tassel. Palace Museum, Beijing.

required to yield, be stern when necessary'. The plume holder was made for a military officer and is dated 1876. Officials and officers of the sixth rank and below were accorded the use of black quills, *lan yu,* from the crow's tail. The one shown on the left in **Figure 1** is protected by a yellow sheath and kept in a flat wooden box. On the bottom of **Plate 4** is a black horsehair plume, used by a military officer in the Manchu banner army, kept in a flat, blue cotton covered box.

Horsehair and silk fringes for winter or summer hats were stored in lacquered or cotton-covered boxes. It was customary during court mourning to remove the red fringing and wear the hat without it for twenty-seven days. A red horsehair fringe at the top of **Plate 4** fits over a central cardboard core and is kept in a blue cotton covered box. The small blue box in the centre contains a short red silk fringe for a winter hat.

Informal Hat

A close-fitting skull cap made of six segments was worn for informal wear by the gentry and for everyday wear by the lower classes. **Figure 2** shows a hat worn by the Guangxu Emperor (ruled 1875–1908) made of dark blue satin, appliquéd with *shou* characters intertwined with butterflies, edged with brocade, and topped with a red silk knot and tassel. Others wore hats made of black satin or gauze and topped with a red or black knotted silk cord knob, which was changed to blue if the wearer was in mourning. The hat

註冊商標
馬
摺帽
精製

was called a *guan pimao*, or melon cap, as it resembled a half melon, or else *xiao mao*, meaning 'small hat'. For summer the hat was often lined with rattan for ventilation. Some hats were stiffened and sold in circular cardboard boxes, but others were soft and folded into six to store easily in triangular boxes or paper pouches. The skull cap continued to be worn well into the middle of the twentieth century, but the shape changed from the earlier flatter crown to a more pointed one. On the left of Plate 5 is a hat in silk gauze over a rattan frame for wear in summer, and on the right a folded black satin cap with its original box.

Some skull caps had a queue or pigtail attached. As a sign of subjugation, all Chinese males had to shave the front of their head and wear their hair in a single plait in the style of the Manchu rulers. Resented at first, it was later accepted and became most respectable. As a punishment, the queue could be cut off, and to be called 'tailless', *wu bian,* was a great insult. At the end of the nineteenth century, when men went to study or travel overseas they removed the queue, so on their return they wore a hat with a false one attached. In fact, however, most queues were lengthened by the addition of some false hair. The wearing of the queue was forbidden after 1912 and soon died out.

From the skull cap developed black satin hoods which buttoned under the chin for wear in the bitterly cold weather of northern China. **Plate 5** shows one lined with fur and another, in the centre, with a quilted floral design lined with black velvet.

WOMEN'S HEADWEAR

Court Hat

Female members of the imperial household also wore the *chao guan* with court dress. At the beginning of the Qing dynasty, both the summer hat and the winter hat were worn, but by the reign of the Kangxi Emperor the winter style was worn throughout the year. It was similar in shape to the men's winter hat, with a fur brim and the crown covered with red floss silk tassels, but with the addition at the back of a flap shaped like an inverted gourd and made of fur. In summer the hat brim and neck flap were faced with black satin or velvet.

There were elaborate gold decorations on the crown, as seen here in **Figure 3** of a first-rank imperial consort's summer *chao guan*. The brim and back flap are in black velvet, and red floss silk fringing covers the crown, while seven gold phoenix ornaments set with pearls are placed around the crown. Lesser imperial concubines wore five phoenixes on the crown. At the back of the hat is a golden pheasant from which three strings of pearls, anchored by a lapis lazuli ornament in the centre, hang down over the back flap. Princesses wore hats with the crown covered with red floss silk and decorated with golden pheasants, while the hats of lower-ranking noblewomen had small jewelled plaques around the base of the crown just above the brim.

Ji Guan

Empresses and imperial consorts wore the *ji guan*, or festive hat, with their dragon robes. It resembled the emperor's winter hat, having red

[PLATE 5]
From the left: a man's silk gauze skull cap; man's quilted hood; man's silk hood lined with fur; "Horse" brand skull cap made in Shanghai folded with its original box. Collection of the author.

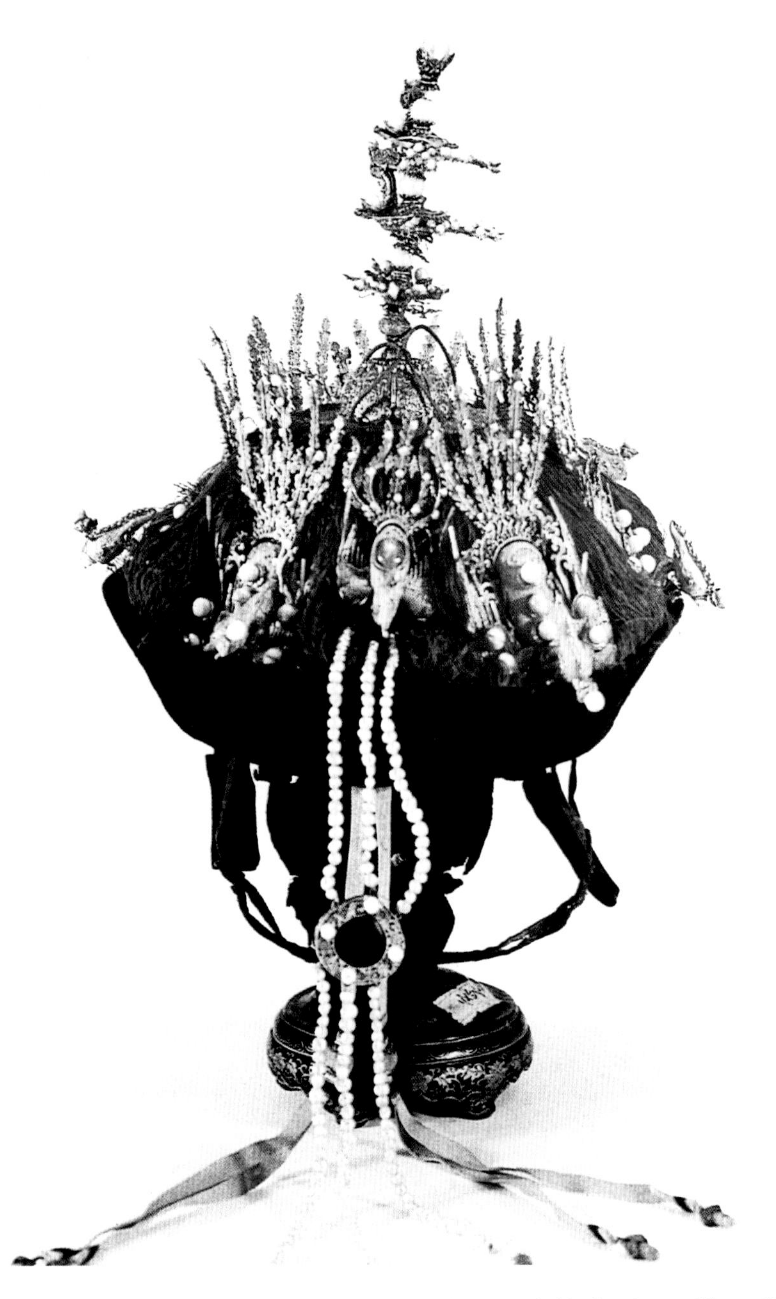

[FIG 3] Above: First-rank imperial consort's summer *chao guan* in black velvet, red floss silk fringing on the crown, and decorated with gold phoenixes set with pearls. National Palace Museum, Taipei.

[PLATE 6] Opposite: A detail from a portrait of the Empress Xiaoxian, first principal consort of the Qianlong Emperor, wearing a *ji guan* topped with a Manchurian pearl.

silk tassels and a fur brim, while for summer the brim was faced with black satin. **Plate 6** shows a portrait of one of the Qianlong Emperor's principal consorts in her dragon robe wearing a *ji guan* topped with a pearl. Around her forehead is a silk band with a jewel at the centre which replaced the gold diadem worn with the court hat.

Lower-ranking noblewomen wore more elaborate hats, the crowns of which were covered with red or blue satin decorated with embroidery or semi-precious stones and topped with a red silk knot on the crown. Two wide embroidered streamers were inserted through a horizontal slit in the brim and hung down the back. **Plate 7** shows a noblewoman's *ji guan* for winter with a black sable fur brim; for summer the brim would be made of black satin. The crown is covered with blue satin and decorated with pearls, jade and other jewels. It has a red silk cord knob at the apex, and the two streamers which fell down the back to below the waist have couched gold dragons on blue satin chasing the flaming pearl. Other designs on the streamers include the Eight Buddhist emblems. Two small bouquets of flowers were sometimes tucked in the hat just above the ears.

Tien Ze

A headdress called a *tien ze* was worn by Manchu women on informal festive occasions. It was made like an inverted basket, with the framework of woven rattan or wire covered with black gauze or silk net and dressed with many jewelled ornaments. **Figure 4** shows a *tien ze* headdress

皇后

of wire lattice woven with black silk ribbon and decorated with kingfisher feather inlay and gold filigree in the style of the Endless Knot, with butterflies and the *shou* character.

Informal Headdress

An unusual headdress called a *liang patou* was worn by Manchu women for non-official occasions. It was a very elaborate affair with the batwing-like shapes made of false hair or black satin arranged over a frame which was anchored with hairpins to the natural hair. Literally meaning 'two handfuls of hair' the hair itself was originally set and shaped this way, but during the nineteenth century hair was replaced by black satin as being more practical and easier to keep in order. As the Qing dynasty drew to a close, the headdress became larger. Artificial blossoms were placed at each side, silk tassels hung down and the whole creation was embellished with jewelled ornaments. However, older women continued to wear a smaller, less elaborate *liang patou,* as seen here in **Plate 8**. This headdress is made of stiffened black satin formed over a cross-piece of gilded silver and mounted on a wire base.

Coronet

Han Chinese women had no prescribed dress rules, but on formal occasions they wore a coronet called a phoenix crown modelled on those worn by empresses in earlier, Chinese-ruled dynasties. **Plate 9** shows a headdress formed over a copper wire base, covered with kingfisher feather inlay flowers, butterflies, phoenixes with pearls and tiny mirrors to deflect bad spirits.

[PLATE 7]
Opposite, top: Noblewoman's *ji guan* for winter with a fur brim. National Palace Museum, Taipei.

[FIG 4]
Opposite, bottom: A *tien ze* worn by Manchu women on informal festive occasions. Palace Museum, Beijing.

[Plate 8]
Below: An informal headdress worn by an older Manchu woman, made of black satin mounted on a wire base. Collection of the author.

[PLATE 9]
Kingfisher feather headdress. Teresa Coleman Fine Arts, Hong Kong.

[PLATE 10]
A wedding coronet made from stamped metal with numerous puff balls, early twentieth century. Collection of the author.

天

Figure 5 shows a bride wearing a jewelled headdress, the numerous strings of pearls concealing her features, which although normally heavily rouged, on this occasion must be white and unadorned. The strings of pearls were not parted until the last moment of the wedding ceremony. A red silk cover for the head and face would also be placed over the headdress to further hide the features of the bride, a tradition which dated back to the Song dynasty (960–1279). Thus doubly covered and concealed in a closed sedan chair, the poor bride would be stifled and shaken on her way to marry a man she had quite probably never met, let alone chosen as her life's partner.

Slightly less elaborate wedding coronets could be hired by the lower classes, along with the collar and the embroidered jacket and skirt for the wedding day. The headdress was made of a kind of plaster of Paris, cloth-covered card or stamped metal, on top of which were beads and sequinned motifs in the form of butterflies, flowers, and phoenixes. Colourful puff balls quivered on wires, pink or red tassels hung at each side, and rows of pearls hung over the front to cover the face, while at the back was a flap with more sequin decoration and tassels. In **Plate 10** the coronet is from southern Guangdong, made from stamped metal with numerous puff balls, and dates to the first half of the twentieth century. **Plate 11** shows a small tiara with puff balls on wires with bells behind them, kingfisher feather inlay phoenixes and flowers, silk flowers, and red glass balls from which hang long silk tassels; it dates from the late nineteenth century.

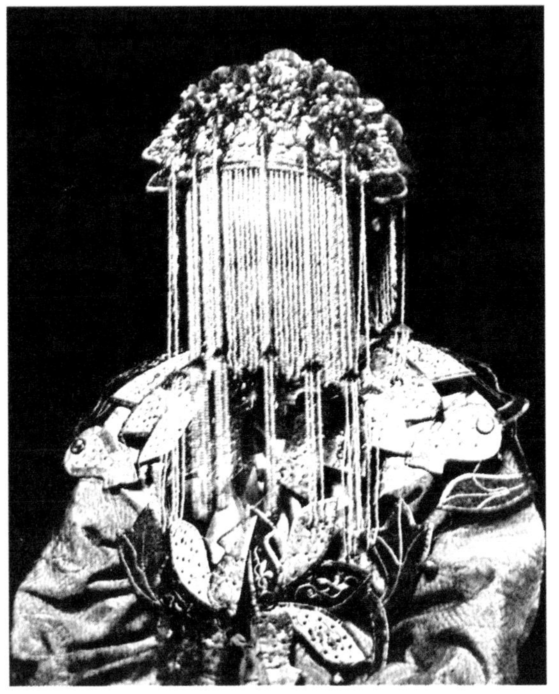

Headband

It was the convention upon marriage for a woman to wear her hair drawn back into a bun at the nape of her neck. As this hairstyle caused the hairline to recede, on reaching middle age the woman would wear a shaped and embroidered band across her forehead for warmth. Only married women wore these bands and they were made or bought as part of the wedding dowry. A group of Chinese ladies in **Figure 6** are wearing voluminous jackets over pleated skirts, their tiny bound feet appearing from underneath; their headbands are embellished with flowers.

Plate 12 shows three headbands. The first has an extended back flap made of yellow silk embroidered in satin stitch showing a lion, butterflies, bats, flowers and two horses over a

[PLATE 11]
Opposite: A small tiara with kingfisher feather decoration and long silk tassels. Collection of the author.

[FIG 5]
Left: A bride, her face obscured by strings of pearls.

[FIG 6]
Above: A group of Chinese women wearing headbands, circa 1900.

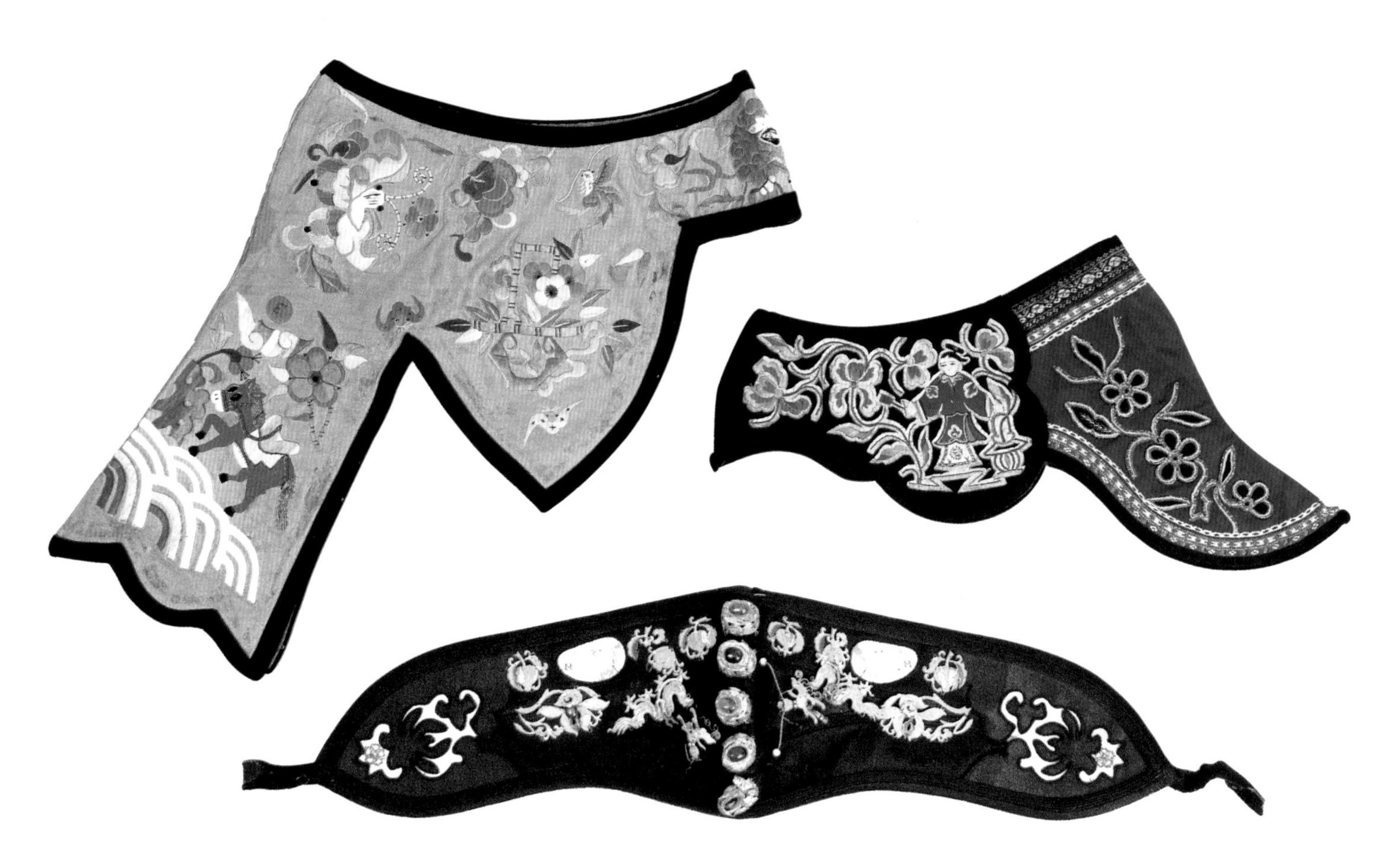

[PLATE 12]
Above: Three different types of headbands. The first is made of yellow silk embroidered in satin stitch; the second has a flap embroidered with a design of plum blossoms; the third is made of black satin decorated with kingfisher feathers and pieces of jade. Collection of the author.

[PLATE 13]
Opposite: Six pairs of ear muffs. Collection of the author.

sea wave border. The second has a short flap embroidered with plum blossoms, while across the front is the design embroidered over a gold paper cut of a scholar on horseback successfully returning from an examination and being greeted by his wife. The third headband is made of black satin with a reverse appliqué design at the sides and decorated with kingfisher feather dragons, jewels and pieces of jade.

Earmuffs

Padded, lined, and shaped like a heart, earmuffs slipped over the ears to keep them warm. Though not confined to either sex or any age group, they were generally worn by girls. They were sometimes trimmed with fur at the edges to represent an animal thought to give protection. **Plate 13** shows six pairs. From the top: a pair in black satin edged with fur, with ties to keep them together; the characters indicate a wish that the earmuffs may keep the ears warm for three winters. Next to them is another pair in black satin edged with fur, this time with flower vases, one holding plum blossoms, the other chrysanthemums, willows and a bowl of flowering narcissi. Below is a pair made of black

能遮两耳寒
不畏三冬冷

satin with a deer, a crane and a cypress tree. Next to them is a pair of purple satin ones with orchids and sacred fungus. On the bottom row is a blue and yellow pair with a fierce-looking animal in the centre; next to it is a pair with five bats around a central *shou* character and with five more bats and five *shou* characters around the edge.

CHILDREN'S HATS

There were several types of hat a child would wear from infancy up to early teens. Young children wore hats for protection against evil spirits and then, as the child grew older, to bring good fortune when taking examinations. Many colourful examples still surface in the antique shops and markets in China.

Rice Bowl Hat

The first style was worn from the age of one month, when it would be presented to the child, usually by the maternal grandmother. Made from a strip of red satin or cotton gathered at the top, it was called a 'rice bowl' style in the south, as it resembled an upturned rice bowl. It was embroidered with designs of flowers, fruit and Chinese characters wishing the child long life and good fortune. In the centre of **Plate 14** is a red silk rice bowl style with amulets across the front depicting the Eight Immortals with Shou Xing in the centre. The *Ba Gua* symbols are embroidered in couched gold thread around the hat. **Figure 7** shows a young boy wearing a rice bowl hat with an amulet at the centre front. His father is wearing the black skull cap.

[PLATE 14]
Below: From the left, open crown in the style of a tiger; a dog head style in red silk; child's rice bowl style; a multi-coloured dog head hat. Collection of the author.

[FIG 7]
Opposite: A boy wearing a rice bowl hat and his father wearing a skull cap, circa 1900.

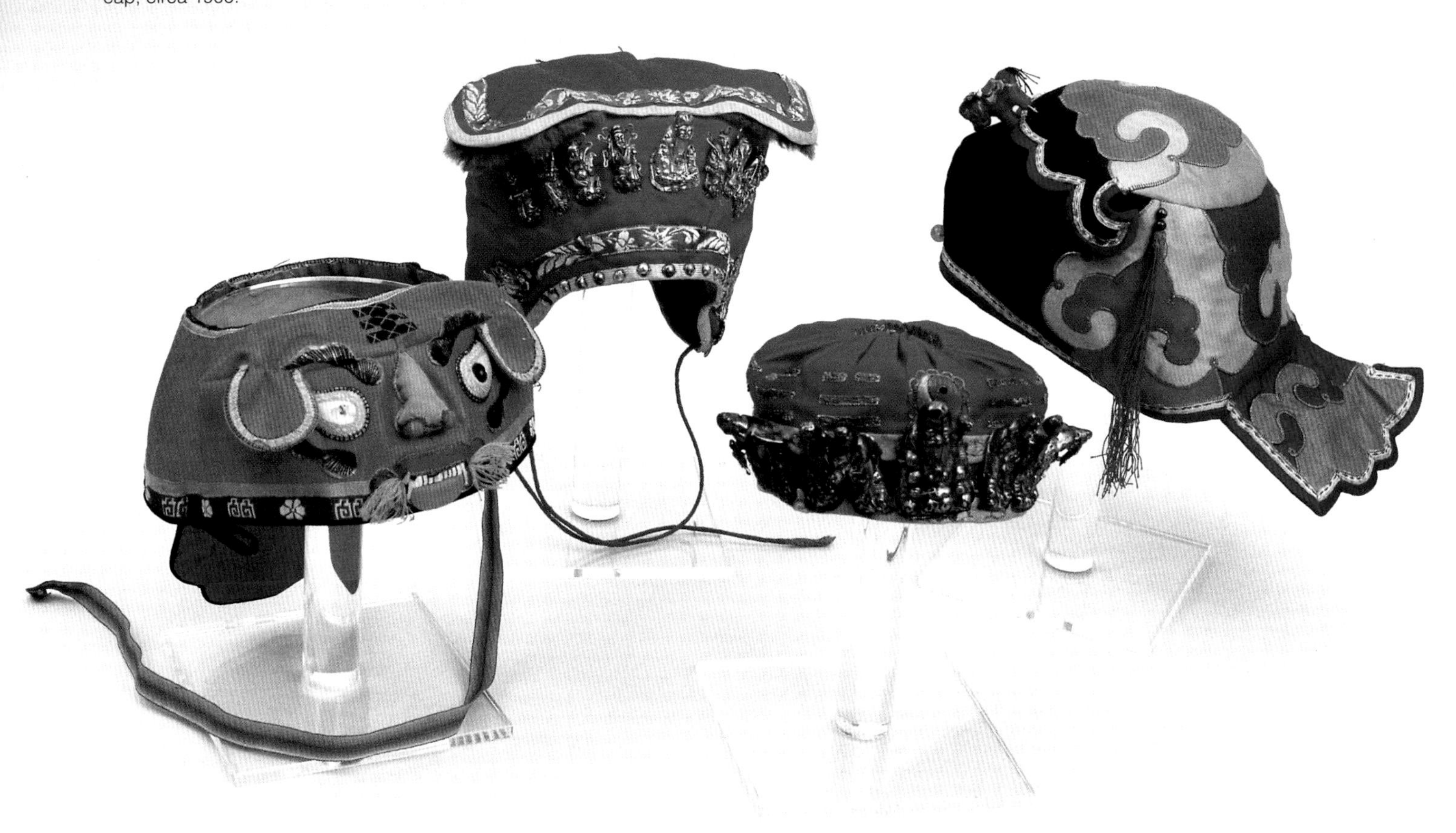

[PLATE 15]
Above: Two wind hats at the left and centre with a hood on the right. Collection of the author.

[PLATE 16]
Opposite: A group of animal hats: from the left a dog with a lion on his back, a tiger wind hat and a *qilin*. Collection of the author.

Open Crown

The second type, also worn in infancy, was similar to the first, but the top of the crown was more open. It often took the form of an animal such as a tiger, lion or pig, with the face at the front and a padded tail at the back. At the left of **Plate 14** is a tiger hat with a backflap embroidered with the Endless Knot. The Chinese character for 'king' is at the centre, the tiger being considered king of beasts.

Dog Head Hat

When the child was about a year old, he would wear a dog head cap to fool bad spirits into thinking the child was an animal and thus of no value. This cap was made of black or red cotton or silk, either plain or patterned. A horizontal cut about a third of the way up from the front was folded down to give the impression of a dog's ears. Next to the tiger hat in **Plate 14** is the dog head style in red silk with 'ears' which have little tufts of fur to further suggest the animal. Across the front is a row of amulets of the Eight Immortals and Shou Xing. The dog head style on the right has multi-coloured satin appliqué in a *ruyi* design with a short back flap to keep the neck warm; there is a tiny padded horse on the top at the front.

Wind Hat

The wind hat was a style for winter wear. Shaped like the dog head hat, or with the crown gathered into a circle, a long back extension kept the neck warm in cold weather. This type was often lined and padded, some being embroidered with flowers and birds, while others had the face of a fierce animal. A long hood was another version of this style; it is seen on the right in **Plate 15**. This one is made of pink silk embroidered with cranes, Buddha's hand and peaches and trimmed with fur. There is a row of nine amulets representing the laughing Buddha across the front: this friendly figure is thought to dispel misery and suffering from the world. Above them are long life amulets. The black satin hat on the left has couched gold thread embroidery of two four-clawed dragons and two phoenixes amid swirling clouds and flames. The third hat, in the centre, has an appliquéd emblem of a bat surrounded by flowers and butterflies.

Animal Hat

The next style to be worn was the animal hat made to represent either a lion, tiger or dog, and

to emulate the strength and ferocity of the animal. All the hats had ears to hear evil approaching, large protruding eyes to spot danger, and a mouth full of bared teeth. Some animal hats had another animal on top of the hat to give greater protection. An embroidered back flap was added to cover the back of the neck in cold weather. Animal hats are still worn in the northern provinces, especially Shaanxi and Shandong.

On the left of **Plate 16** is a double hat, a lion riding on the back of a dog with a wind flap. The dog was always shown in black, while the lion was usually green with a long silky mane. Another animal, seen on the right, is the *qilin*, with the two horns extended, flames issuing from its nostrils and a ball suspended from its mouth, while on its back is a child riding a tiger. The tiger wind hat in the centre has a padded tail in orange satin marked in this case with 'eyes' or else black stripes; there are tiny mice in each ear.

Scholar Cap

As the boy grew older, hats were worn less to protect against evil, and more to bring success for the future. Such was the reason for the scholar cap, given to the child in the hope that he would do well in the official examinations. At the back were often two streamers and two pointed 'feathers' which had been on the gauze caps worn by scholars and officials during the Ming dynasty. These are seen in **Plate 17**, while the front of the crown is embroidered with cranes and flowers, with the Endless Knot around the brim.

Crown

Hats worn on festive occasions and for the Lunar New Year were shaped more like a crown. One type, called an eagle hat, had upturned wings said to represent an eagle which, as it soared high, ensured the wearer would rise high in office; as it swooped low, suggested the wearer would live to become a grandfather. The one in **Plate 17** is made of pink silk and couched gold thread embroidery of flowers, deer and the *shou* character, with long pink tassels at each side and green streamers at the back.

[PLATE 17]
Opposite: A scholar's hat and a crown. Collection of the author.

Eight Segment Hat

Another style was the hat with a false fringe and queue made of black twisted silk thread. The crown was made of stiffened cardboard, covered with silk, and divided into eight sections, each embroidered, often with emblems of the Eight Immortals.

Skull Cap

A final style, for everyday use, was the plain black skull cap, like those worn by men. The cap was made from six segments fixed to a narrow brim. Made of stiffened black satin, it was topped with a black or red button or silk pom-pom.

Endnotes

[1] Verity Wilson, *Chinese Dress*, Victoria & Albert Museum, London, 1986, p. 27.

[2] Verity Wilson, *Chinese Dress*, p. 28.

~ *Chapter Four* ~

Jewellery

In many cultures jewellery is seen as a means of displaying wealth and status, while for the poor it is a way of dressing up simple attire for special occasions. In China, as an important indicator of rank, it was listed in the Regulations and thus affected members of the imperial family, both male and female, and officials in the Manchu government. Men wore certain items of jewellery as a symbol of learning and scholarship, while for Chinese women it demonstrated the affluence of the family. Another significant function of the many jewelled charms worn especially by children was as protection against evil and to ward off unwelcome influences. Jewellery was given to the child by family members and friends, usually at a celebration held at the first month after the birth. This is still the custom in many parts of China.

Silver, gilded silver, brass and gold were the base metals. Gold jewellery was a form of investment and a means of saving. The pure metal was stamped with the jeweller's mark, thus binding him by guild law to buy the article back at any time by weight. Silver was not as prized and was often gilded to look like gold and stop it from tarnishing. Pure silver was very soft. Much of the jewellery worn by the less well-to-do was made of an alloy resembling silver known as *bai tong*, or white copper, which was copper containing a small amount of zinc and nickel.

Jewellery was decorated or inlaid with enamel, bone or ivory, or precious and semi-precious stones such as jade, coral, turquoise, rose quartz, lapis lazuli, ruby and sapphire. Certain stones were worn in the wintertime, like jade, coral and agate. Cedar and carved ivory were brought out in hot weather.[1] Other materials included tortoiseshell, shagreen and soapstone.

In particular, jewellery inlaid with kingfisher feathers was very popular, the fashion dating back to the Tang dynasty. Called *tsae mou*, or the laying-on of feathers, the delicate work of cutting the feathers with a chisel into the size and shape required, then gluing them onto the base metal, took many hours for one item. Wedding head-dresses, haircombs, pins and earrings were made from these iridescent blue feathers. They were produced in great quantities for the domestic market, as well as many pieces for export to Europe, the last ones being made as recently as the 1930s in a Guangzhou workshop. These feather inlays are naturally very delicate and fell off easily; recent examples of newly restored pieces are coming on the market and can be identified by the newer, brighter feather inlay on the original metal base.

[PLATE 18]
Chinese girl wearing hair ornaments, earrings, bracelets, pendant charm and rosary, circa 1800.

CHART 1

Insignia on Imperial *Chao Guan*

RANK	NO. OF TIERS	NO OF DRAGONS	NO. OF EASTERN PEARLS	JEWEL OF RANK
Emperor	3	12	13	precious pearl
Crown prince	3	12	13	eastern pearl
Emperor's son	2	4	10	ruby
First-rank prince	2	4	10	ruby
Son of a first-rank prince	2	2	9	ruby
Second-rank prince	2	2	8	ruby
Third-rank prince	2	2	7	ruby
Fourth-rank prince	2	2	6	ruby
First-rank duke	2	2	5	ruby
Second-rank duke		2	4	ruby

Source: Dickinson & Wrigglesworth, 1990

CHART 2

Hat Insignia for Official's *Chao Guan*

RANK	1636 JEWEL	1645 JEWEL	SMALLER SETTING
First	ruby	ruby	pearl
Second	ruby	ruby	red
Third	ruby	ruby	blue
Fourth	sapphire	sapphire	blue
Fifth	crystal	crystal	blue
Sixth	crystal	crystal	–
Seventh	gold	chased gold	blue
Eighth	gold	chased gold	–
Ninth	–	chased silver	–
RANK		**1730-1911 JEWEL**	**SMALLER SETTING**
First		ruby	pearl
Second		coral	red
Third		sapphire	blue
Fourth		lapis lazuli	blue
Fifth		crystal	blue
Sixth		white jade	crystal
Seventh		plain gold	crystal
Eighth		chased gold	–
Ninth		chased silver	–

Source: Dickinson & Wrigglesworth, 1990

JEWELLERY FOR MEN

Hat Insignia

Laws for the hat insignia worn by Manchus date back to 1636, before the overthrow of the Ming dynasty, for the purpose of having an easily visible means of identification of the different ranks of officials. Later, these laws were codified and set down in the Regulations. Jewelled finials were worn at the top of the summer or winter hat. They were more conspicuous than rank badges, especially as the badges were only worn on 'Full Dress' occasions; at other times a plain surcoat was worn. Reports of the time usually refer to the mandarin as, for instance, 'the wearer of the blue button', omitting to mention the bird or animal on the rank badge.

Imperial Family

The insignia worn by members of the imperial family was in the form of a tall gold finial intricately decorated with dragons, Buddhas and tiers of pearls, the number of tiers dependent on the importance of the man within the family (Chart 1). Chapter 3, **Plate 2** shows a summer hat belonging to the Qianlong Emperor. The hat finial of gold dragons and sixteen Manchurian pearls exceeds the number prescribed in the Regulations, and many surviving finials differ in some way.

Mandarin's Hat Finial

Hat finials were worn by officials on ceremonial occasions. They were fixed to the apex of the crown by a long metal screw which passed through a hole in the hat. Above the ornamental base was a spherical shape with a small setting of transparent stone or a piece of glass, then above that the tall jewel depicting rank. At first the tall jewel was rounded and smooth, *en cabochon*, but later in the nineteenth century the Chinese learnt the art of faceting the stones, and the flashing colours gave maximum impact to the rank.

The colours of the jewels were based on the Manchu banners. The flags of the military divisions were red, blue, white and yellow. These laws were laid down in 1636, when the court in Shenyang split the civil and military officials into four ranks. After the conquest of China, when the Manchus took over the Ming system of nine ranks, the small settings were added to depict the principal and the subordinate ranks. Then in 1730 the Yongzheng Emperor added opaque stones to the transparent ones already in use in order to denote subordinate rank (Chart 2).

An interesting silver hat finial for a prince or nobleman's military helmet is shown in **Plate 1**. The ruby jewel is *en cabochon* above two vertically facing dragons. It has a cloud collar set with small rubies that may have replaced the pearls as designated. **Plate 2** shows a hat finial for a third-rank official, with a faceted tall blue glass jewel and a small red jewel set in the sphere that may have replaced a blue stone.

Hat Sphere

Hat spheres, sometimes called 'mandarin buttons', were introduced in 1727 by the Yongzheng Emperor to be worn on less formal occasions in order to avoid confusion of rank when the insignia squares were not worn or when

[PLATE 1]
A rare finial for a prince or nobleman's military helmet: red glass jewel above two vertically set dragons with ruby jewels mounted on a silver cloud collar. Ken Rutherford.

[PLATE 2]

Left: Third-rank official's hat finial with faceted blue glass jewel and a small red jewel set in a gilded silver base. Ken Rutherford.

[PLATE 3]

Above: Hat sphere for a fifth-rank official: a crystal knob with an unusual collar of small crystal beads around the base. Ken Rutherford.

CHART 3

Hat Insignia for Official's *Ji Guan*

RANK	1727-30 JEWEL	1730-1911 JEWEL
First	coral (or ruby if permitted)	coral or opaque red glass
Second	coral with engraved *shou* character	coral or opaque red glass with engraved *shou* character
Third	as above	sapphire or clear blue glass
Fourth	lapis lazuli	lapis lazuli or opaque blue glass
Fifth	as above	crystal or clear glass
Sixth	crystal	moonstone or opaque white glass
Seventh	gold	plain gold or gilt
Eighth	gold	gold or gilt with an engraved *shou* character
Ninth	gold	silver until 1800, then gold or gilt with an embossed *shou* character

belt plaques, which also indicated rank, were covered by the surcoat. The emperor was to wear a twisted knob of red silk cord on his semi-formal hat, while noblemen and officials wore a simpler form of round hat jewel (Chart 3). The Regulations were revised in 1730 and incorporated later into the *Huangchao liqi tushi*, which stated that a large baroque pearl in a gold collar could be worn by the emperor and heir apparent on the semi-formal hat. At this point the knot of red silk cord seems to have been reserved for the informal hat.

The Regulations also stipulated that glass could be used instead of semi-precious stones both to save expense and because glass itself was highly prized. **Plate 3** shows a fifth-rank official's hat knob of crystal with an unusual decorative collar of small crystal beads around the base of the sphere.

Scholar's Hat Finial

Graduates of the civil service examinations wore a hat finial with an eagle on top instead of a jewel. The eagle, as it soars high, symbolises rising rapidly in rank; as it swoops low, it represents a desire for long life. For graduates of the first degree, the bird was made of silver, or of *bai tong* as shown in **Plate 4** (page 67); it is 11 centimetres tall with an eagle perched on a sphere with a small red stone setting at the front. Graduates of the next examination at the provincial level, *ju ren* (promoted men), wore the ornament made of silver with a gold bird on top. The metropolitan graduate, *jin shi* (finished scholar), wore a gold ornament with a branch of nine leaves at the top.

Public Servant's Finial

Attendants to the emperor wore other types of hat finials. Court musicians wore yellow feather finials; military posturers who performed a martial dance wore the trident, and civil posturers who performed a slow rhythmic dance at annual sacrifices performed by the emperor wore a flaming jewel, either a ruby or a pearl. **Plate 5** shows the finial belonging to a civil posturer. It is made of gilded silver, the centre pearl surrounded by a turquoise flame motif.

[PLATE 5]
Hat insignia for a civil posturer made of gilded silver, the centre pearl surrounded by a turquoise flame motif. National Palace Museum, Taipei.

Holders for Peacock Plumes

Feather plumes, previously mentioned in Chapter 3 as being awarded on merit by the emperor, were attached to the apex of the hat by a tube made either of semi-precious stones, such as jade or coral, or of malachite, cloisonné or enamel. The one shown in **Plate 4** is made of jade with a silver mounting which was anchored to the apex of the winter hat by the screw of the hat button which passed through the opening in the mounting. Others, especially for summer hats, were attached by a red silk cord through a hole at the top of the tube.

[PLATE 6]
Girdle to be worn by an emperor with the dragon robe. National Palace Museum, Taipei.

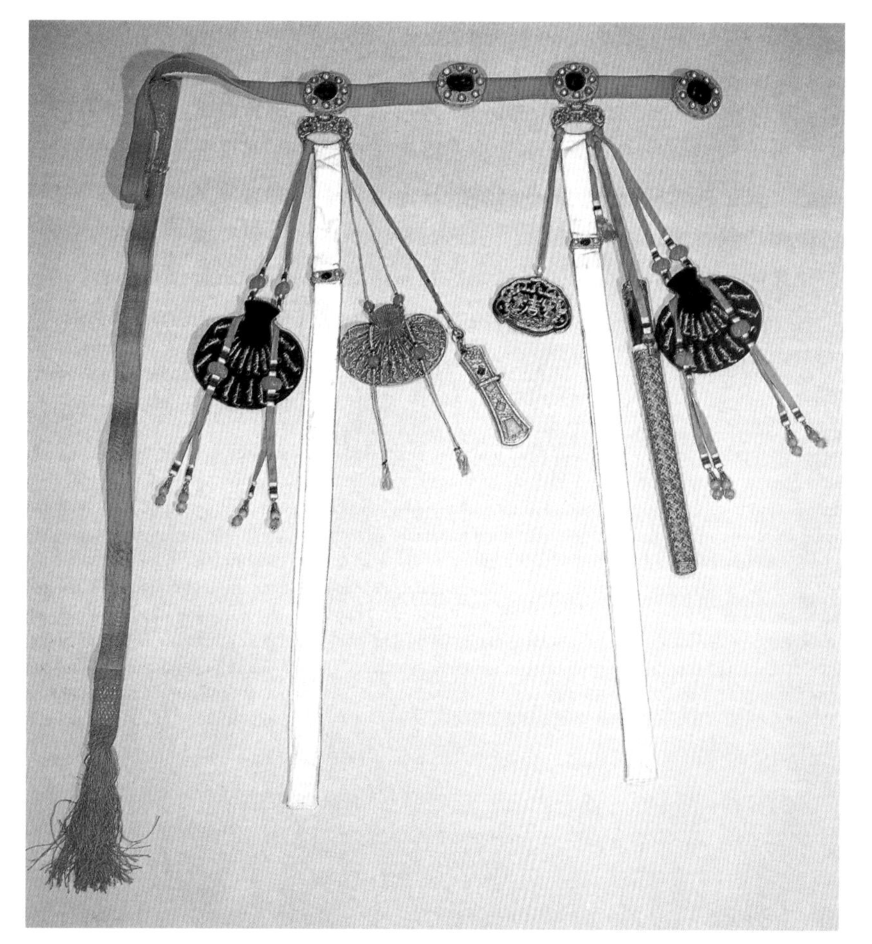

Girdles and Girdle Plaques

There were no pockets in the robes, and girdles made of tightly woven silk were worn closely belted over the robe around the waist to carry articles which were frequently needed. These girdles, *chao dai*, were also a symbol of status and thus were mentioned in the Regulations, the colours being appropriate to the colour of the robe and the rank of the wearer. The emperor and his descendants wore shades of yellow, while mandarins wore blue or blue black silk. Two silk ribbons or ceremonial kerchiefs hung from the girdle. When worn with the court robe the kerchiefs were wide and pointed at the end; when worn with the dragon robe they were narrow and straight, as seen in **Plate 6**. Because the Manchus were formerly a nomadic race, it is thought that the girdle and kerchiefs were originally made of a stronger material, such as woven hemp, and could have replaced a broken bridle if necessary.

A hooped leather belt with jewelled plaques had been worn by the Ming rulers, and the Manchu court continued using ornamental plaques on the girdles as another important form of rank identification. Four ornamental plaques were made of gold or silver set with semi-precious stones or other materials, the centre one being an interlocking belt buckle (Chart 4).

The side plaques usually had oval metal rings at the bottom used to carry a selection of daily essentials, such as a pair of drawstring purses, a fan case, tobacco pouch, chopsticks and knife in

[PLATE 4]

Hat insignia for a graduate of the first degree made in *bai tong* with a small red jewel at the front. Collection of the author. Holder for a peacock plume made of jade with a silver fitting to attach to the apex of the winter hat. Collection of the author.

CHART 4

RANK	GIRDLE CLASP FITTINGS (1645–1911)
First	Four jade rectangular plaques mounted in gold each set with one ruby
Second	Four engraved gold circular plaques each set with one ruby
Third	Four engraved gold circular plaques
Fourth	Four engraved gold circular plaques mounted in silver
Fifth	Four plain gold circular plaques mounted in silver
Sixth	Four tortoiseshell circular plaques mounted in silver[2]
Seventh	Four plain silver circular plaques
Eighth	Four clear ram's horn circular plaques mounted in silver
Ninth	Four black horn circular plaques mounted in silver

Source: Cammann, 1953

[PLATE 7]

Opposite: Set of mother-of-pearl girdle plaques mounted in silver. Peter Tang.

a case. The yellow silk girdle in **Plate 6** was made for an emperor and has four gold plaques set with lapis lazuli surrounded by eight pearls. Drawstring purses hang down from the side plaques with Manchu script detailed in seed pearls and gold beads on the two outer purses and with Peking knot embroidery on the inner purse. A knife purse, a compass purse and a toothpick case are also attached.

The rare set of four mother-of-pearl plaques and the interlocking buckle in **Plate 7** could have been for a sixth rank mandarin, as mother-of-pearl was listed as being for the sixth rank in the late nineteenth century.[3] Although tortoiseshell was the designated material, a shortage may have forced the choice of other materials at this time. So few full sets of plaques have survived that it is difficult to be certain.

There are quite a number of interlocking belt clasps to be found, made of a variety of precious and semi-precious materials. These buckles would have been used on the belt when informal dress was worn and wealth, not rank, was displayed.

Mandarin Chain

Early Manchu emperors had been devout Buddhists and entertained the Dalai Lama lavishly. A Buddhist rosary sent in 1643 by the Dalai Lama to the first Qing emperor, Shunzhi (ruled 1644–1661), developed into the *chao zhu*, sometimes referred to as a mandarin chain, which was worn as part of official dress by members of the imperial family and officials, first as a mark of piety, later as decoration and status.

The necklace had 108 small beads; four large beads of contrasting stone known as *fo tou*, said to represent the four seasons, were placed between groups of 27 beads. Three counting strings of ten beads arranged in two sets of five beads each were also added by the Manchus, and were worn with two strings on the left and one on the right. On the *fo tou* bead between the counting strings was a long drop extension called a *bei yun* (back cloud), that hung down the back and served as a counterweight as well as an ornament. Originally used to keep track of the number of times the prayers were recited to Buddha, these chains were later used in place of an abacus for rapid and discreet calculations, especially useful for mandarins on duty.

The *Huangchao lishi tushi* details who should wear the *chao zhu* and how it should be worn.

The colour of the cords on which the beads were strung must correspond to those of the girdle. Only the emperor could wear 'eastern pearls', i.e. freshwater pearls from Manchuria, but other members of the imperial family, civil officials of the fifth rank and above, and military officials of fourth rank and above, could wear any semi-precious stones they wished. These included amber, jade, lapis lazuli, filigree enamel and carved woods, among others, though many chose glass, as a chain of good jade beads cost as much as £1,000 in 1878.[4] The one shown in **Figure 1** is made of amber with four large jade beads and lapis lazuli counting strings and counterweight. After the fall of the dynasty many chains were broken up and restrung as necklaces for sale to the western market.

The chain was kept in a round box covered in either leather or blue silk. Circular red lacquer boxes with an open centre were also used, and sometimes the base of the hat box had a container for the beads.

Rosary Bracelet

Ancestor portraits often show officials fingering the mandarin chain like worry beads. But rosary bracelets which helped the faithful keep count of the prayers recited to Buddha were also carried or slipped round the wrist, and served the additional function of soothing the nerves. Eighteen beads were divided into nine on each side of a head bead and an anchor bead. Semi-precious stones such as jade, amber, coral or tourmaline, fragrant woods such as cedar or sandalwood, and inlaid silver on bone or wood were used, with the head and anchor beads made of a contrast material.

[FIG 1]
Left: Mandarin chain of amber beads interspersed with four jade beads, the counting strings and counterweight of lapis lazuli. Collection of the author.

[PLATE 8]
Right: Archer's thumb ring of carved wood. Collection of the author.

Archer's Thumb Ring

The thumb ring was originally a leather band worn by archers to assist in drawing the bow. The archer drew "the string back with his thumb, the forefinger being bent over the end to strengthen the hold, and the arrow being held in the crotch made by the junction of the forefinger and thumb. In this method a ring is worn on the thumb to engage the string and to prevent the thumb from being lacerated."[5] Later the ring became an ornament worn by the literati, first on the right thumb, and then on both thumbs. Such was the importance of the thumb ring that on his birthday, when the emperor gave presents to invited guests at a feast, among the gifts of vases and scroll paintings would be archers' rings.

Measuring between 2 and 3 centimetres wide, the ring was made of tourmaline, gutta percha (a tough resin obtained from a variety of

[PLATE 9]
Noblewoman's hat finial of brass with amber jewels. Collection of the author.

Malaysian tree), wood or jade. One of a pair with its own matching case is shown in Chapter 6, **Plate 13**. The ring made of carved wood in **Plate 8** has designs of flowers, fruit, coins and other auspicious symbols.

JEWELLERY FOR WOMEN

Hat Insignia

Surviving examples of women's hat insignia are quite rare, as they were only worn by female members of the ruling Manchu family and noblewomen. As ordained by the Regulations, the hat finial on the *chao guan* worn by the empress, the empress dowager and first-rank imperial consorts was formed of three tiers of golden phoenixes and pearls, as seen in Chapter 3, **Figure 3** on a summer court hat. Lesser-ranking imperial concubines wore finials with two tiers of phoenixes and pearls. Lower-ranking noblewomen wore a simpler, smaller version of the man's hat spike. The one seen in **Plate 9** is made of brass and amber and would have been sewn to the hat through the tiny holes around the base, like the scholar's hat finials, instead of being fixed with a long screw through the crown.

Diadem

The court hat rested on a diadem, *jin yue,* which encircled the forehead. This diadem was also an indicator of rank and appears in the Regulations following the hat. Women in the imperial family wore one made in several sections of gold inlaid with precious stones, such as lapis lazuli and pearls, as seen in **Plate 10**. Although not shown here, strings of pearls would hang down the back, either five or three strings depending on rank, anchored at the top and just above midway by two oval plaques.

Mention should be made here of the diadem worn by lower-ranking women, from wives of dukes down as far as wives of seventh-rank mandarins. This was a band of black satin, about 7 centimetres wide at the centre, decorated with a dragon and phoenix chasing a flaming pearl. Two pendants embroidered in similar fashion hung down the back. Tiny loops at the top attached them to a jewelled hairpin, which was pushed into the hair just under the back fastening of the headband. The one shown in **Plate 11** was for a mandarin's wife and is decorated with four-clawed, profile crouched gold and silver dragons, one either side of a flaming pearl. On each of the pendants, which are 65 centimetres long and 9 centimetres wide at the base, there is a coiling dragon and phoenix of a similar design.

Torque

This jewelled collar is also listed in the Regulations and was worn around the neck by members of the imperial family and noble-women when wearing court dress. Called a *ling yue*, it was made of gold or silver gilt inlaid with semi-precious stones, such as pearls, coral, rubies and lapis lazuli, the number of stones determining rank. Silk braids, the colours corresponding to those of the robes, hung down from the back opening, ending in drop pendants of matching stones. The one shown in **Plate 12** has pearls, kingfisher feathers and coral inlaid in a gold band.

[PLATE 10]
Diadem of gold inlaid with lapis lazuli and pearls. National Palace Museum, Taipei.

[FIG 2]
Below: Page from the *Huangchao liqi tushi* chapter on dress for the empress and empress dowager, showing the style of *zai shui*.

Zai Shui

Another symbol of rank listed for women in the Regulations was the *zai shui*. This was a long, pointed kerchief made of yellow, red or blue silk and embroidered with auspicious emblems, such as the dragon and phoenix. Suspended from a jewelled ring, it fastened to a centre button on the court vest or to the side top button on the dragon robe. Silk cords with charms made from jade or other semi-precious stones hung from the jewel, with a jewelled bar approximately one-third down from the top. Seen in **Figure 2** is a page from the volume of the Regulations covering dress worn by the empress and the empress dowager. This *zai shui* is designed for the empress, to be embroidered in green and other colours with the Abundant Harvest of the Five Grains pattern on a bright yellow ground.

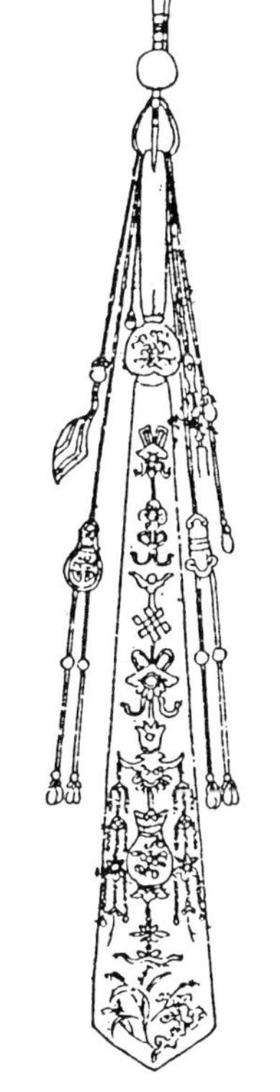

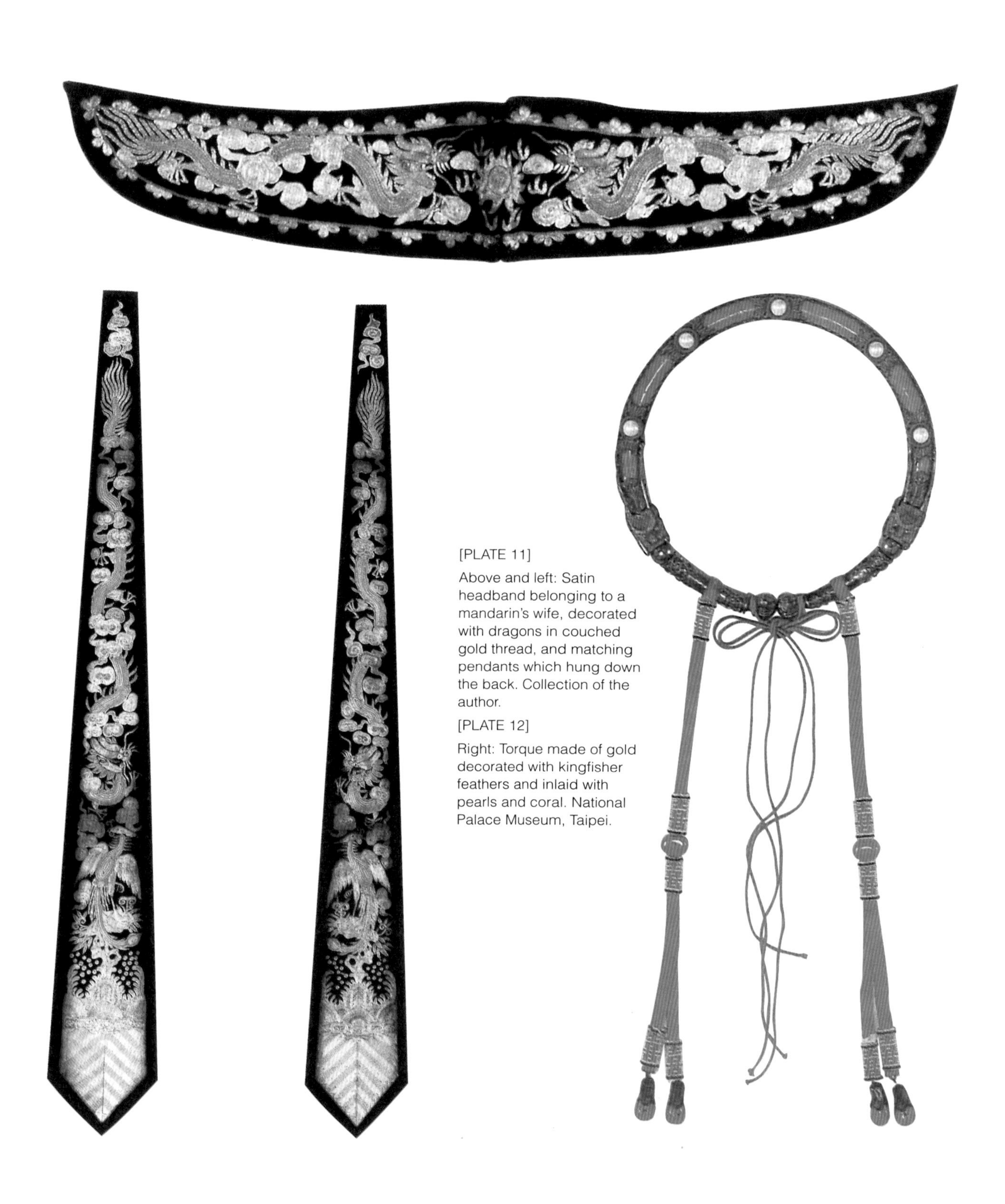

[PLATE 11]

Above and left: Satin headband belonging to a mandarin's wife, decorated with dragons in couched gold thread, and matching pendants which hung down the back. Collection of the author.

[PLATE 12]

Right: Torque made of gold decorated with kingfisher feathers and inlaid with pearls and coral. National Palace Museum, Taipei.

The same design was permitted to imperial consorts and consorts of princes, while the ones worn by princesses and noblewomen were plainer. The one in **Plate 13** is made of blue silk with embroidered flowers and butterflies; small charms are suspended from the top jewel.

A narrow band of silk about 100 centimetres long and 7 centimetres wide, embroidered with auspicious symbols and decorated with jewels, was worn by women in the imperial family with informal dress. It looped around the neck, with one end tucked into the top of the gown. This can be seen in Chapter 6, **Figure 1** worn by the Empress Dowager, the wife of the Guangxu Emperor (on her right), and one of her ladies-in-waiting.

[PLATE 13]
Kerchief, or *zai shui*, made of blue embroidered silk hung with gold enamelled charms. National Palace Museum, Taipei.

Mandarin Chain

The female members of the imperial family, noblewomen, and wives of the high officials also wore a *chao zhu*, or court necklace, with court dress. Women were required to wear two other necklaces crossing from left shoulder to right underarm, and vice versa, as well as the main one which hung down the front. However, when wearing the dragon robe on semi-formal occasions just one necklace was worn.[6]

Only the empress or empress dowager could wear eastern pearls for the main necklace, while the other two necklaces were made of coral. Imperial consorts wore amber for the main string and coral for the two secondary strings, while consorts below the third degree wore coral for the principal chain and amber for the other chains. The remaining ranks could wear any type

of semi-precious stones, except those that were restricted. **Figure 3** shows Wan Rong, wife of the Xuantong Emperor (ruled 1909–1912), in a photo taken at the time of their marriage in 1922, wearing three court necklaces, together with a *zai shui* attached to the button on her court vest, a diadem, torque, earrings, and hat finial with three phoenixes.

Women also carried hand beads which were a smaller version of a single court chain, but rosary bracelets like those carried by men were more common. The charming one in **Plate 14** is of tourmaline beads in delicate shades of green, pink and turquoise, the drop with rows of tiny seed pearls.

Earrings

The final pieces of jewellery to be listed in the Regulations were earrings, *erh-shih*. Women from the imperial family and Manchu noblewomen had pierced ears and wore three pairs of drop earrings in each ear when wearing court dress. These were made of pearls set in gold and can be seen in the portrait in Chapter 3, **Plate 6**.

Han Chinese women also had pierced ears and wore earrings made from a variety of semi-precious stones, such as gold, jade, coral and pearls, with kingfisher feather inlay to form auspicious emblems. Shown later in **Plate 21** are a pair of hooped earrings made of silver with a design of bats and flowers, circa 1900.

Hair Ornaments

Across the top of the Manchu woman's huge winged headdress, that was worn on less formal

[FIG 3]
Left: Wife of the Xuangtong Emperor wearing court dress at her wedding, including the *zai shui*, torque, diadem, earrings and three mandarin chains.

[PLATE 14]
Opposite: Woman's rosary bracelet of green, pink and turquoise tourmaline beads. Teresa Coleman Fine Arts, Hong Kong.

occasions, was a flat hairpin called a *pien fang*, or crosspiece, over which the hair was arranged and separated, as seen in Chapter 3, **Plate 8**. When hair was replaced by black satin in the late Qing period, the *pien fang* helped secure the headdress to the real hair. The hairpins were about 30 centimetres long and 3 centimetres wide, and made of many materials, including jade, gold, enamel and tortoiseshell. Auspicious designs, including longevity characters, flowers and bats, were depicted. The hairpin in **Plate 15** is made of gold engraved with a design of acanthus leaves. The smaller one is also engraved on gold, but made for the Han Chinese woman's

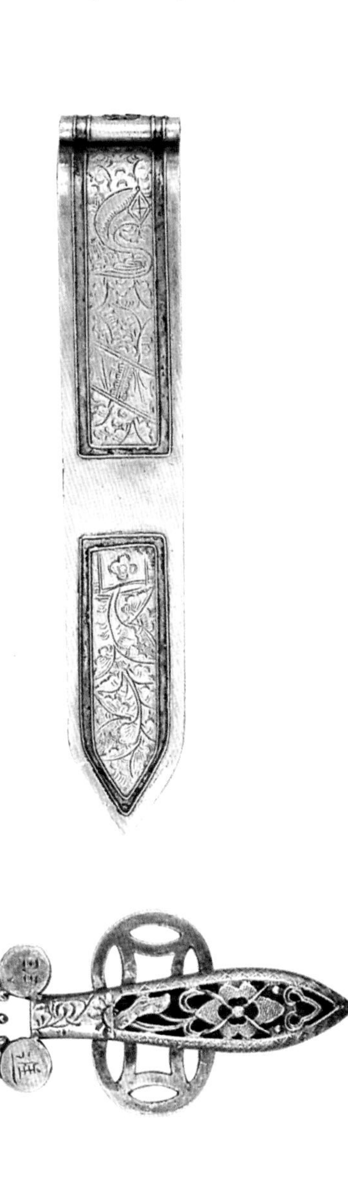

[PLATE 15]
Gold cross piece, Manchu. Collection of the author. Gilded silver hair pin, Han Chinese. Teresa Coleman Fine Arts, Hong Kong. Hairpin given as approval for a wedding; 1900. Yesteryear, Hong Kong.

[PLATE 16]

Opposite: Kingfisher feather hairpins. Collection of the author/Teresa Coleman Fine Arts, Hong Kong.

[PLATE 17]

Above: Seen from above, two silver and blue enamel hairpins. Teresa Coleman Fine Arts, Hong Kong.

hairstyle. The small hairpin at the bottom is of gilded silver. It was given to the prospective bride by her future in-laws as a sign that the marriage, in all likelihood arranged by a matchmaker, could go ahead. The design is of coins, flowers and a bat holding two circles containing the characters *jun mun*, literally 'enter door'.

Han Chinese women wore their hair in upswept styles held in place by a jelly-like liquid, made from a certain kind of wood shavings steeped in water, which was brushed through the hair. When set, this mixture held every strand in place. Into this stiff arrangement a large number of hairpins were put, made of gold, enamel, silver, or semi-precious stones such as jade or coral and fashioned into insects, birds or butterflies. Many were made of kingfisher feather, as shown in **Plate 16**, in the form of bats, butterflies and flowers. The pair in **Plate 17** are in silver with blue enamel leaves surrounding flowers and butterflies. **Plate 18** (page 60) shows a young Chinese lady, her hair decked out with jade and coral hair ornaments, wearing earrings, bracelets and a pendant charm, with a rosary slipped behind the top button at the right shoulder of her gown.

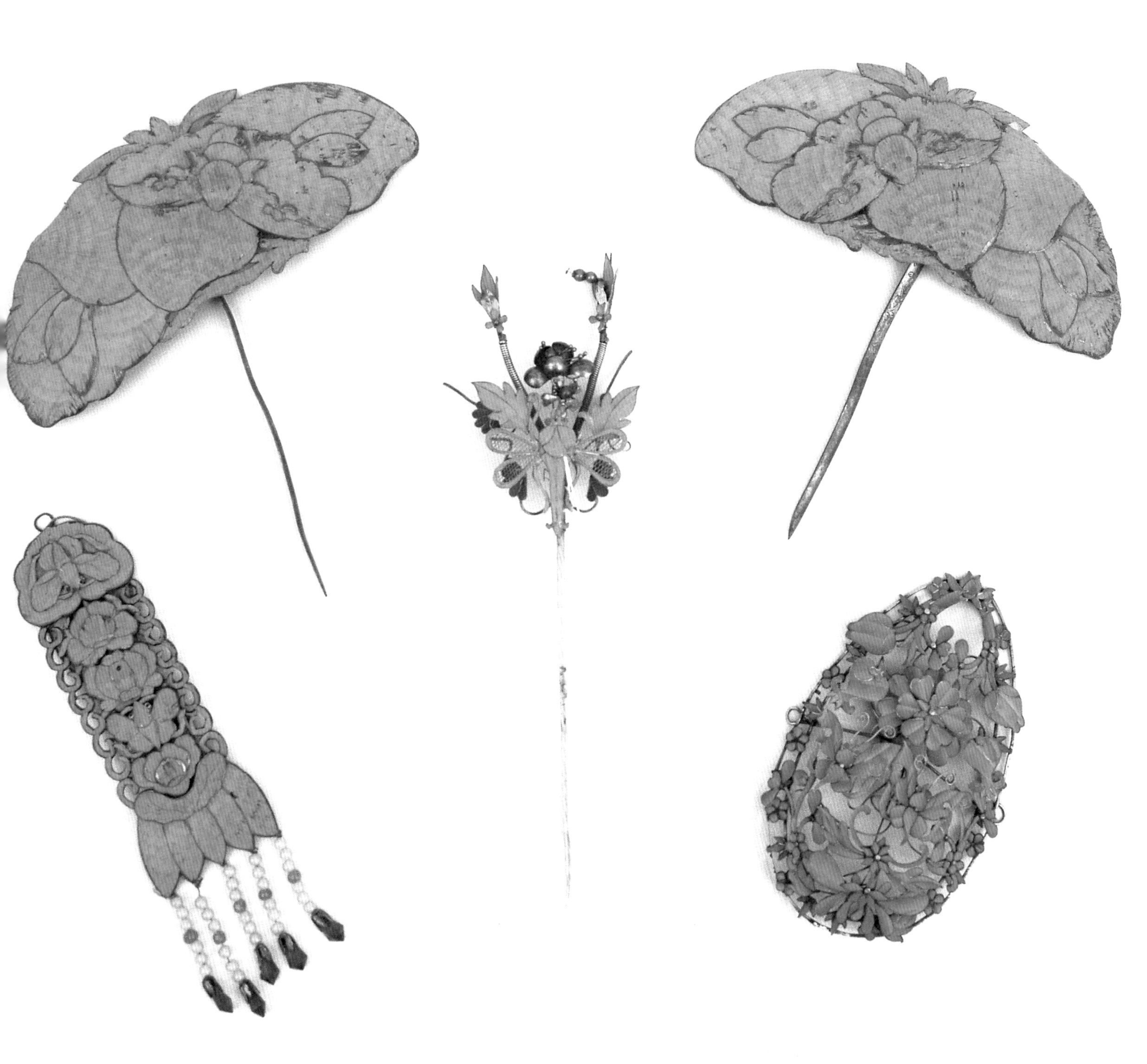

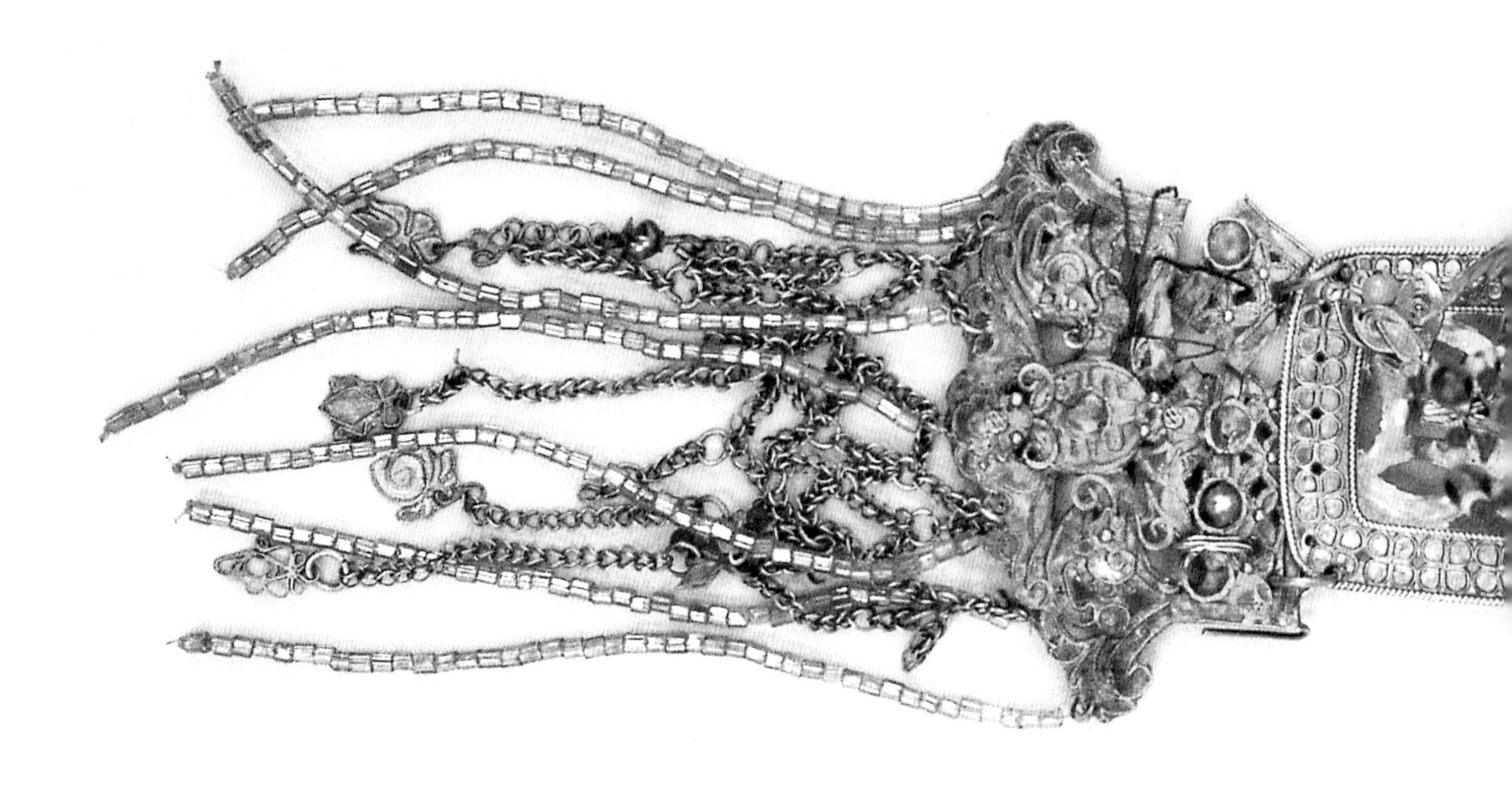

[PLATE 19]
Gilded silver hairpin set with glass jewels worn by a fisherwoman at her wedding in the 1930s. Collection of the author.

Large sets of hairpins were given as part of the dowry on marriage. The one shown in **Plate 19** was part of a set of thirty-five elaborate hairpins acquired by a fisherwoman in southern Guangdong in the 1930s as part of her dowry. Made of gilded silver, studded with glass jewels, they are intricately worked in designs of coins, insects, flowers and butterflies.

Other Items of Jewellery

Bracelets and anklets were generally worn in pairs made of gold, silver, enamel, horn, ivory, fragrant woods, jade, and other semi-precious stones decorated and inlaid with similar materials in the design of flowers and auspicious emblems. Some were hollow with small beads inside to produce a rattling noise when moved. **Plate 20** shows a group of silver ornaments: a pair of bracelets carved with designs of birds and flowers; two combs; a pendant made to contain potpourri, with an openwork design on the front showing a laughing child, coins, bats and flowers, with hanging charms of cockerels and a fish; and a pair of anklets with hanging peach stone charms with bells inside.

The other item in **Plate 20** is a needle case

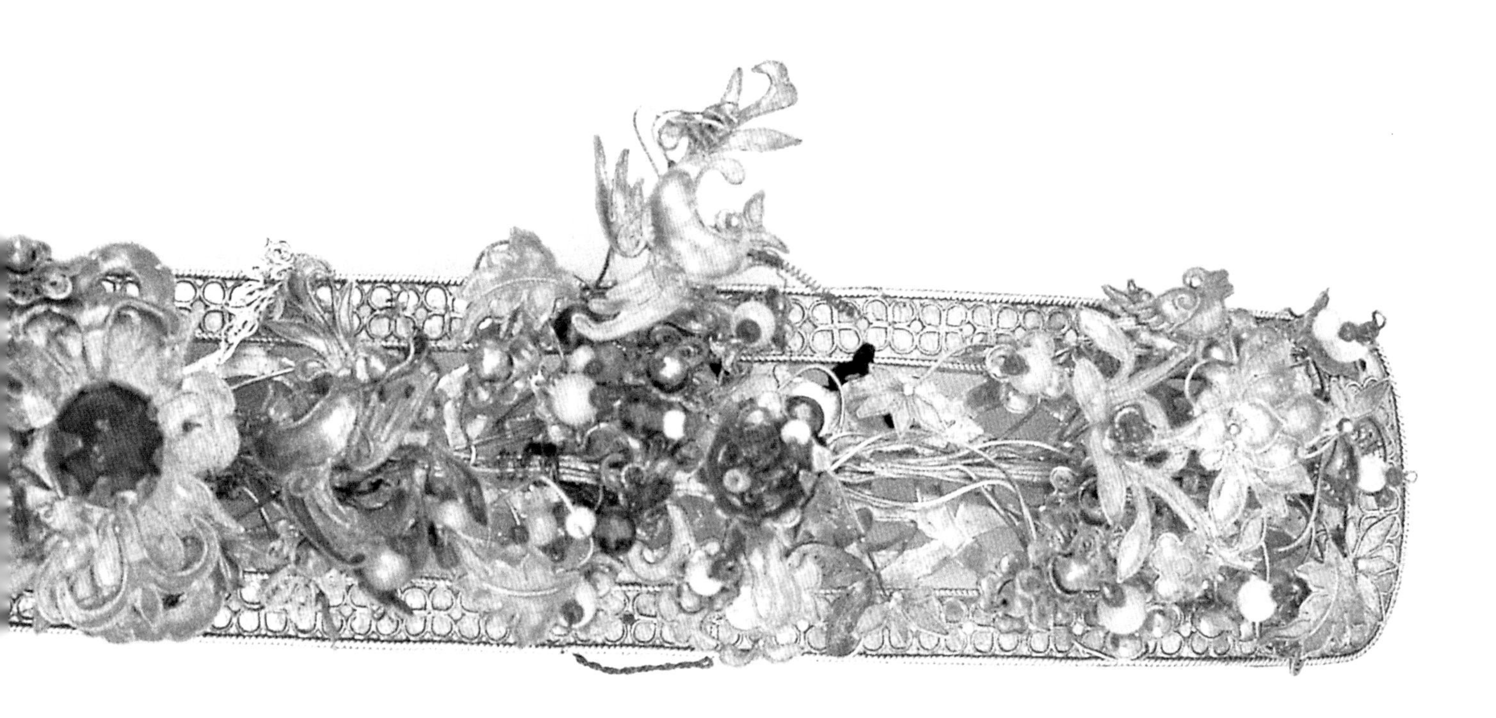

decorated with figures in the procession of a successful graduate. Needle cases were made of *bai tong* or silver, often enamelled, and were carried pinned to the gown or attached to the top side button. Originally needles were made of ivory, bone, bamboo or porcupine quills. Later, in the nineteenth century, when steel needles were imported from Germany, they were expensive and needed to be kept in a safe place.

Equally elaborate rings were made of enamel, jade, gold and semi-precious stones inlaid with various stones. **Plate 21** shows a silver ring with the character for long life in the centre.

Most people of gentility cultivated at least one long nail to show they did not engage in manual work, and nail guards were worn by women to preserve the treasured nail, though men did not use them. They were about 7 centimetres long, made of gold, silver gilt, enamel or tortoiseshell, in filigree designs of coins, longevity symbols and other symbols. Women often wore two different pairs on each hand, on the third and fourth fingers. **Plate 21** shows one of silver engraved with two Daoist emblems.

Elaborately carved silver chatelaines were carried fastened to the top button on the upper

[PLATE 20]

Above: Silver jewellery, including a pair of bracelets, two combs, pendant, anklets, and a needle case. Teresa Coleman Fine Arts, Hong Kong.

[PLATE 21]

Opposite: Silver earrings for a Han Chinese lady, circa 1900, Yesteryear, Hong Kong. Silver ring with the *shou* character, Teresa Coleman Fine Arts, Hong Kong. Silver nail guard, collection of the author.

[PLATE 22]

Left: Silver chatelaine with three implements, Yesteryear, Hong Kong. Long silver pendant with small bell charms. Teresa Coleman Fine Arts, Hong Kong.

[FIG 4]

Above: Chains worn around the neck with the *doudou*. The outer one made of silver with dragons on the coins, the inner one made of *bai tong* with lions for the fastenings. Collection of the author.

garment. They had sets of three or five chains hanging from a central plaque, ending with a selection of the following: tongue scraper, toothpick, nail cleaner, earpick or snuff spoon, and tweezers (which were also useful for making the knotted fabric ball buttons). The chatelaine shown in **Plate 22** is made of silver and has an earpick, nail cleaner and toothpick and two peach stone charms hung from a floral plaque. Pendant charms made of jade, amber or gold were also hung from the top side button on the gown and can be seen in **Plate 18**, while a longer one, seen in **Plate 22**, is made of silver with little bells which tinkled as the wearer moved. Other pendants, as in **Plate 20**, were made of filigree metal like a potpourri container, and held fragrant herbs to sweeten the air. Little hanging mirrors, embroidered at the back under glass were popular in the late nineteenth century. Another unusual hanging plaque was the abstinence badge worn suspended from a button on the robe. Members of the Manchu court, male and female, wore them on the days leading up to an important sacrificial ceremony as a reminder to abstain totally from wine, strongly flavoured spicy foods, music and sensual pleasures.[7] The badges, which were made of materials such as gold inlaid with turquoise, amber, jade, enamel and sandalwood, were rectangular, oval or gourd-like in shape, between 5 and 10 centimetres high and 3 to 6 centimetres wide. On one side were the Chinese characters *zhai jie,* meaning 'fast' or 'abstinence', with the equivalent in Manchu script on the reverse (**Plate 23**).

Silver chains were worn around the neck, with fastenings slipped into loops on the chest cover, or *doudou*. In **Figure 4**, the outer chain is made of silver and has three link chains held by coins bearing four-clawed dragons on the obverse, the ends of the chain having butterfly hooks. The inner chain is made of *bai tong* with lions at each end to cover the hooks.

JEWELLERY FOR CHILDREN

Chinese children wore many charms as a means of protecting them from harm. The God of Longevity was a popular amulet to be hung

[PLATE 24]
Silver padlock for a child; silver anklet with bell charms. Teresa Coleman Fine Arts, Hong Kong. Child's amulet in *bai tong* of Shou Xing riding a *qilin*. Collection of the author.

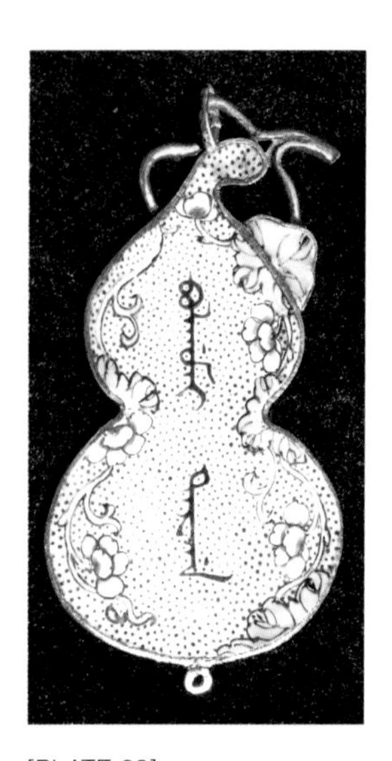

[PLATE 23]
Abstinence badge in enamel with Manchu script, and Chinese characters on the reverse, reminding the wearer to abstain from sensual pleasures and to undergo ritual purification in the days before an important sacrificial ceremony. Marilyn Gardner Hamburger.

around the child's neck. He was depicted either mounted or standing beside a deer or *qilin*, holding the peach of immortality in one hand and a staff in the other. The *qilin* was often used as an auspicious symbol for children, as it was thought to have great wisdom, as well as symbolising a desire for a large family of sons who would do well in the Civil Service examinations. It is shown at the bottom of **Plate 24** made of *bai tong*. A jade Buddha is another charm still popular today which is worn suspended around the neck during childhood.

Amulets stamped out of a thin sheet of silver or brass were frequently stitched across the front of the child's hat. A set of the popular Eight Immortals can be seen on two of the hats in Chapter 3, **Plate 14** together with the God of Longevity, Shou Xing, in the centre. It is said the Eight Immortals and Shou Xing were guests of the Queen of the Western Heavens at her birthday feast. One or more Laughing Buddhas were also placed across the front of the cap and are shown also in Chapter 3, **Plate 15**. He is a friendly figure believed to be able dismiss misery and unhappiness from the world. Other amulets displayed Chinese characters for good fortune and long life, and especially the *Ba Gua*, also known as Eight Trigrams.

Bells were worn in the hope that their noise would scare off bad spirits, and were part of the sets of charms given to the baby at the first month celebration. They were also attached to the cap strings at the back of the hats. A single large brass bell was tied to the ankle with red string, or else anklets were worn made of jade or silver with charms containing bells hanging from them, as seen in the centre of **Plate 24**. Bracelets made of jade or silver were worn around both wrists and continued to be worn when an adult.

A very common tradition was the wearing of a padlock made of silver or *bai tong* inscribed with propitious characters and symbols around the neck to 'lock the child to earth'. Padlocks like the silver one in **Plate 24** with a scene of a child carrying a *ruyi* and riding on a *qilin* were sometimes attached to a chain, or else joined to the neck ring, as shown in **Figure 5**. This large silver ring with a padlock and peach stone charms was large enough to go over the child's head. It was meant to be the equivalent of a dog collar and intended to fool the evil spirits into thinking the child was an animal, and therefore of no value.

Endnotes

1 Hilda Arthurs Strong, *A Sketch of Chinese Arts and Crafts*, China Booksellers, Ltd., Peking, 1926, p. 184.

2 In a letter to the author dated Feb. 14, 1991, Cammann writes of the sixth rank being tortoiseshell set in silver, which would be more logical than his previous description of it set in gold.

3 J. Dyer Ball, *Things Chinese*, 1892, reprinted Oxford University Press, Hong Kong, 1982, p. 365.

4 C. Gordon Cumming, *Wanderings in China*, William Blackwood & Sons, London, 1888, p. 52.

5 Edward Morse, *Glimpses of China and Chinese Homes*, Little, Brown, Boston, 1902, p. 131.

6 Schuyler V.R.Cammann, *Ch'ing Dynasty* "Mandarin Chains," *Ornament*, Vol IV, no 1, 1979, p. 26.

7 For more on these fascinating but rare jewelled plaques, see Teresa Tse Bartholomew, "Abstinence Badges from the Wiant Collection," *Orientations*, Nov. 1993, pp. 79–84.

[FIG 5]
Child's silver neck ring with padlock and peach stone charms. Collection of the author.

~ Chapter Five ~

Collars, *Xia Pei* and *Doudous*

COLLARS

Before the beginning of the twentieth century, robes, whether sumptuously decorated with dragons for official occasions or made of plain silk for informal events, had a collarless neck opening finished simply with a narrow band. To add importance when necessary, a detachable collar was worn on top.

Pi Ling

A flared shoulder collar known as a *pi ling* was shown together with the court robe in the Regulations for both men and women. The collar is thought to have developed from a hood worn by the Manchus before the conquest, which had been opened out along the top of the crown to extend beyond the shoulders.[1] It either attached to the top button of the court robe or fastened independently. Although intended for wear only with the court robe, photographs and paintings show it was also worn with the dragon robe and the surcoat bearing the rank badge when 'Full Dress' was required.

The *pi ling* was made to match the robe and embroidered or woven in brocade or *kesi*. Dispersed across the main field were dragons, *long* or *mang* according to rank, above a sea wave base. Men wore collars with five dragons, with two in profile on each side and one front-facing in the centre back. Women's collars had two profile dragons which were placed on either side of the mountain. In the background were clouds and lucky emblems. A narrow embroidered border containing more clouds and auspicious emblems was surrounded by a wider, plain border all the way around the edge which corresponded to the edging on the court robe.

The summer court robe was trimmed with brocade, and so was the *pi ling*, as seen here in **Plate 1**. This is a man's collar; the edge is trimmed with a wide border of gold brocade, and the five *mang* dragons are embroidered in satin stitch. The first style of winter court dress worn by the emperor and high officials was deeply trimmed with fur, so the *pi ling* was completely covered with fur. The second style of winter court robe had the edges trimmed with fur, and so had the *pi ling*. The wife of the Xuangtong Emperor is shown wearing one with full court dress in Chapter 4, **Figure 3**.

Ling Tou

Early Qing portraits of female members of the imperial family show them wearing a small fur collar with the dragon robe. During the second half of the nineteenth century, it became the fashion for men of rank to wear a similar small, plain, stiffened collar called a *ling tou*, which fitted

[PLATE 2]

Opposite: Lady's official collar in counted stitch on silk gauze of the *shou* character surrounded by the Eight Buddhist emblems, eighteenth century. Jobrenco Ltd, Chris Hall Collection Trust.

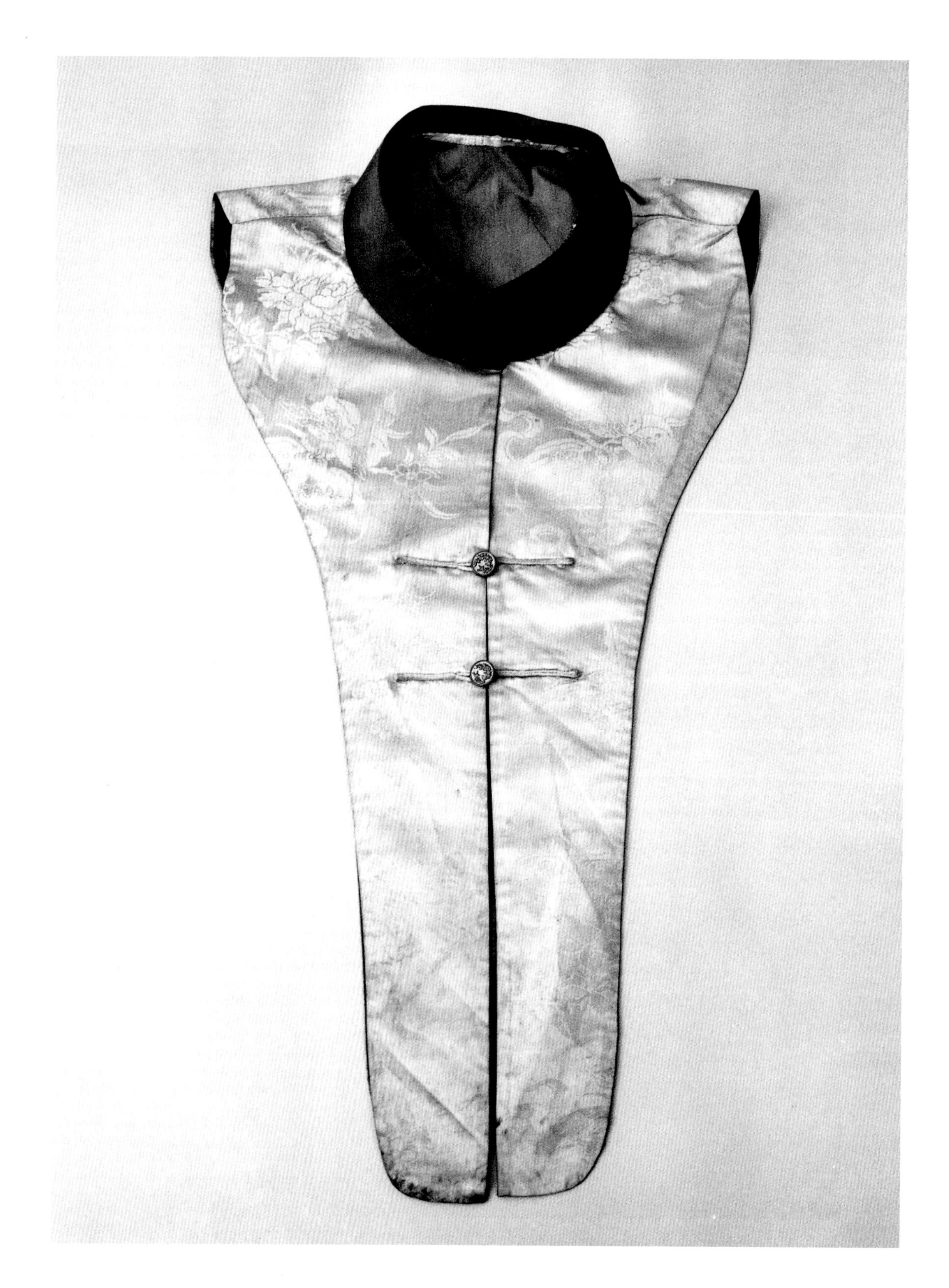

[FIG 1]
Ling tou made of silk.
Collection of the author.

over the neck of the surcoat or jacket when worn with the dragon robe or informal robe. The collar band was made of dark or light blue silk, velvet, or fur, according to the season, mounted onto a narrow shaped neckband. When the *ling tou* was made of silk or velvet it had an extended piece which buttoned at the front and hung down at the back. This was worn inside the robe. The extended piece was a different colour from the collar, as seen in **Figure 1.** Here the *ling tou* has a deep blue silk collar with a pale blue silk brocade extended piece lined in a deeper blue. The collar part fastens with hidden hooks and eyes, and there are flat brass buttons and loops in the middle of the extended piece. *Ling tou* are quite scarce because they were plain, and thus earlier collectors of Chinese embroidery and textiles saw no reason to acquire them.

Cloud Collar

The *yun jian,* or cloud collar, was worn by Han Chinese women for formal occasions, especially weddings, hence it is often referred to as a wedding collar. It is a detachable four-pointed collar which was worn over the *mang ao,* or dragon jacket, by a bride on her wedding day and at other times after marriage for formal or official occasions. In **Figure 2** the collar is made of red silk, considered an lucky colour by the Chinese. The four lobes at chest, back, and over each shoulder indicate the cardinal points, with the wearer's head forming the cosmic centre. Each lobe is shaped like the *ruyi,* and in each of the four cardinal points are fish, bats, lions and other symbols, all embroidered in Peking knot.

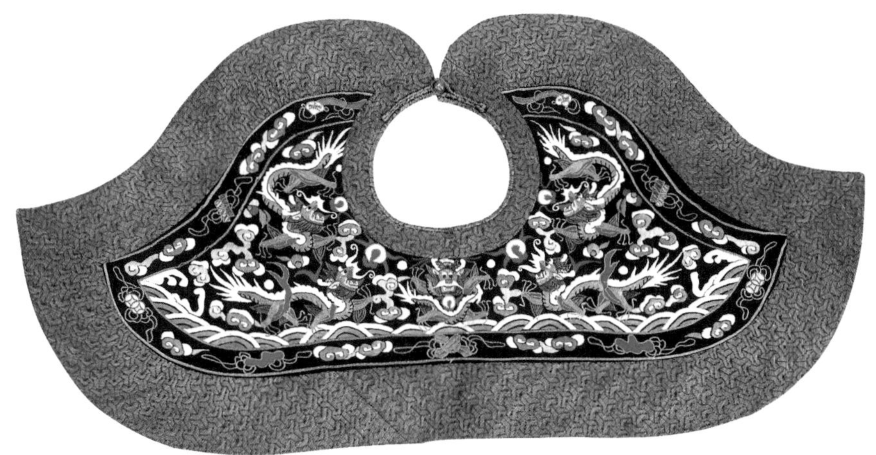

The collar in **Plate 2** would probably have been worn by an older woman when presiding with her husband on official occasions; it dates from the eighteenth century. The design, in counted stitch on silk gauze, is of the *shou* character surrounded by the Eight Buddhist emblems; in the four corners around the neck is the double *dorje*, a very powerful Buddhist emblem that gave the wearer invincibility and impregnability against demons.

Other multi-lobed collars had many petals which radiated from the neckband and fell over the shoulders. The painting from the Guangzhou

[PLATE 1]
Above: *Pi ling* for a man with five four-clawed dragons embroidered in satin stitch. The wide border is of brocade, and the collar would have been worn with a summer court robe. Collection of the author.

[PLATE 3]
Below: Painting by the Guangzhou artist Tinqua, circa1850, shows a group of women wearing multi-lobed collars.

[FIG 2]

Yun jian, or cloud collar, of red satin with auspicious symbols embroidered in Peking knot, nineteenth century. Collection of the author.

[PLATE 4]

Opposite: Wedding collar with a design of peonies, pomegranates, fish and bats embroidered in Peking knot and couched gold thread; circa 1800. Teresa Coleman Fine Arts, Hong Kong.

[PLATE 5]

Multi-lobed wedding collar, mid-nineteenth century. Teresa Coleman Fine Arts, Hong Kong.

studios of the artist Tinqua of a birthday celebration in the mid-nineteenth century (**Plate 3**) shows four women wearing multi-lobed collars. Some collars were very highly decorated, with many tassels. They were usually made in three layers, in cream, red and blue, or cream, peach and green. **Plate 4** shows a wedding collar dated to around 1800 which is covered completely with Peking knot outlined with couched gold thread. The design is of peonies in a vase at the centre back, two fish at the centre front opening, four bats around the neck and pomegranates over each shoulder. The radiating lobes around the neck are all embroidered in couched gold thread. The collar in **Plate 5**, dated to the mid-nineteenth century, in shades of cream and blue-green silk, has multiple segments outlined in black in the shape of the *ruyi* and the bat. The centre motif shows a scholar being presented with his degree.

Children's Collars

Infants and young children wore collars made of several segments, usually five or six, while some were elaborately subdivided into many smaller sections, each segment decorated with auspicious symbols. In **Plate 6** six embroidered bats encircle the neck, each attached to a cloud motif. The one on the right has auspicious fruits embroidered on silk: the pomegranate, peach and Buddha's hand, as well as persimmon, an emblem of joy. On the left of **Plate 7** is a collar, possibly made for the son of a mandarin, in a circle with a design of two four-clawed dragons chasing a flaming pearl against a background of clouds and mountains. The one on the right has five segments, with two birds and three animals: the horse, the deer and the lion.

In the northern provinces, collars were often shaped like a fierce animal's body, particularly the lion or tiger. When the collar was put on, the animal appeared to be coiled around the child's neck, giving greater protection. **Plate 8** shows a very colourful tiger next to a lion decorated with sequins and embroidery. These fierce animals have certain features in common: large eyes to spot evil lurking, a prominent nose to sniff it out, alert ears, and a mouth with teeth bared ready to devour the evil; claws are also well-defined.

Another popular motif is a smiling child in the form of a collar, as seen in **Plate 9**. The other shows five boys each wearing a collar, *doudou*, trousers and jacket: obviously a desire for a large and happy family.

XIA PEI

So far, all emblems of rank discussed have related to members of the imperial family or officials working for the ruling Manchu government. But wives of Han Chinese officials wore their own symbol of status: a ceremonial vest, or *xia pei*, which had antecedents dating back to the fifth century A.D. During the Ming dynasty, female members of the imperial family and wives of officials wore an embroidered neck stole on ceremonial occasions. The stole, which hung down over the chest, was decorated with dragons and birds or flowers, according to rank.[2]

During the Qing dynasty the stole developed into a wider, sleeveless tabard which fastened

[PLATE 6]

Children's collars: one with six bats encircling the neck; one with four auspicious fruits. Collection of the author.

[PLATE 7]

Children's collars: one a circle with a design of four-clawed dragons, the next of five segments, each containing a symbolic animal or bird. Collection of the author.

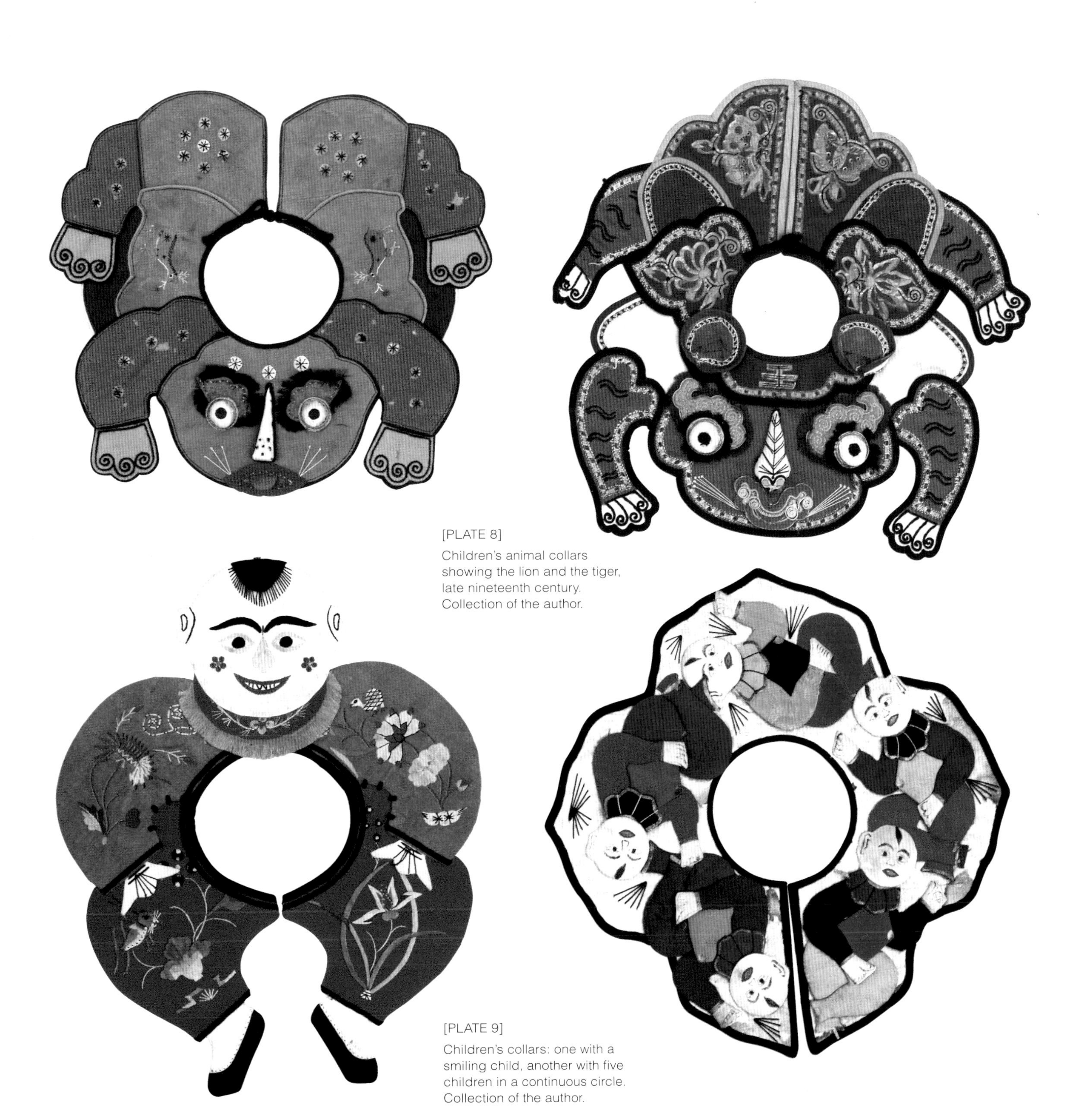

[PLATE 8]

Children's animal collars showing the lion and the tiger, late nineteenth century. Collection of the author.

[PLATE 9]

Children's collars: one with a smiling child, another with five children in a continuous circle. Collection of the author.

[FIG 3]

The two wives of a mandarin, photographed in 1898 wearing the *xia pei*.

with tapes at the sides, reaching to below the knee and finishing, later in the dynasty, with a fringe at the pointed hem. The regimented decoration became more general and was dispersed around the *xia pei*. Profile dragons and *li shui* were added to the skirt part, and on the chest and back was a space for the badge of rank, which corresponded to that worn by the husband. The two wives of a mandarin in **Figure 3** were photographed in 1898. The bird on the rank badges on their *xia pei* is carefully concealed by the sleeves of their jacket, intending to imply a higher rank.

The *xia pei*, like the robes, could be embroidered or made of *kesi* or brocade. It was first worn on the wedding day over the *mang ao*, or dragon jacket, then afterwards at events of special importance connected with the husband's rank. A cloud collar with the four lobes at chest, back and over each shoulder, was incorporated into the *xia pei*, or else worn separately over the upper garment. **Plate 10** shows a red silk *xia pei* embroidered in red, blue, green, yellow and white, with two profile dragons at the neck and skirt part on the front and one front-facing dragon at the neck and skirt part on the back, all worked in couched gold thread. The insignia badges are incorporated into the garment at chest and back. They show an egret, symbol of the sixth civil rank, in a natural setting, as befits the style of the Qianlong period.[3] Surrounding the badges are the Eight Buddhist emblems. **Plate 11** shows a later *xia pei*, from the middle of the nineteenth century, made of dark blue silk with couched gold thread dragons and birds from the nine different civil ranks embroidered in Peking knot. The insignia badge shows the wild goose, symbol of the fourth civil rank, also embroidered in couched gold thread and Peking knot.

There was another kind of *xia pei* worn by Manchu women of high rank. This was a full-length sleeveless vest with a ground colour of yellow, green, white and possibly other colours as well, with profile ascending dragons, edged with a velvet band and brass studs. The deep fringe at the hem, which is lined behind, suggests a hybrid garment which developed from the Chinese women's *xia pei*.

DOUDOU, OR CHEST COVER

A *doudou* was a small triangular apron worn next to the skin to cover the breasts and stomach. It developed from a bodice worn during the Ming dynasty, and continued to be worn by women and children up to the early years of the twentieth century. The apron was narrow at the neck with a wide curved or pointed base, and was held to the body by a silver chain or tape around the neck and waist. At the base of the apron was sometimes a pocket stretching the full width of the garment. Those made of silk were in red, or shades of red, while those of cotton were usually black or natural colour. *Doudou* were richly embroidered with auspicious symbols, as they were especially close to a woman's heart. Some were plain on the outside, but underneath was a secret inner flap with a painting of an erotic scene.

Plate 12 shows a red silk *doudou* made for a wedding. The embroidered central motif of a heavenly maiden carrying a child and riding on a *qilin* is a wish for the birth of a son who will

[PLATE 10]

Opposite: *Xia pei* in red silk with the dragons worked in couched gold thread and a sixth rank civil badge; Qianlong period. Teresa Coleman Fine Arts, Hong Kong.

[PLATE 11]

Blue silk *xia pei* with a fourth rank civil badge, circa 1850. Collection of the author.

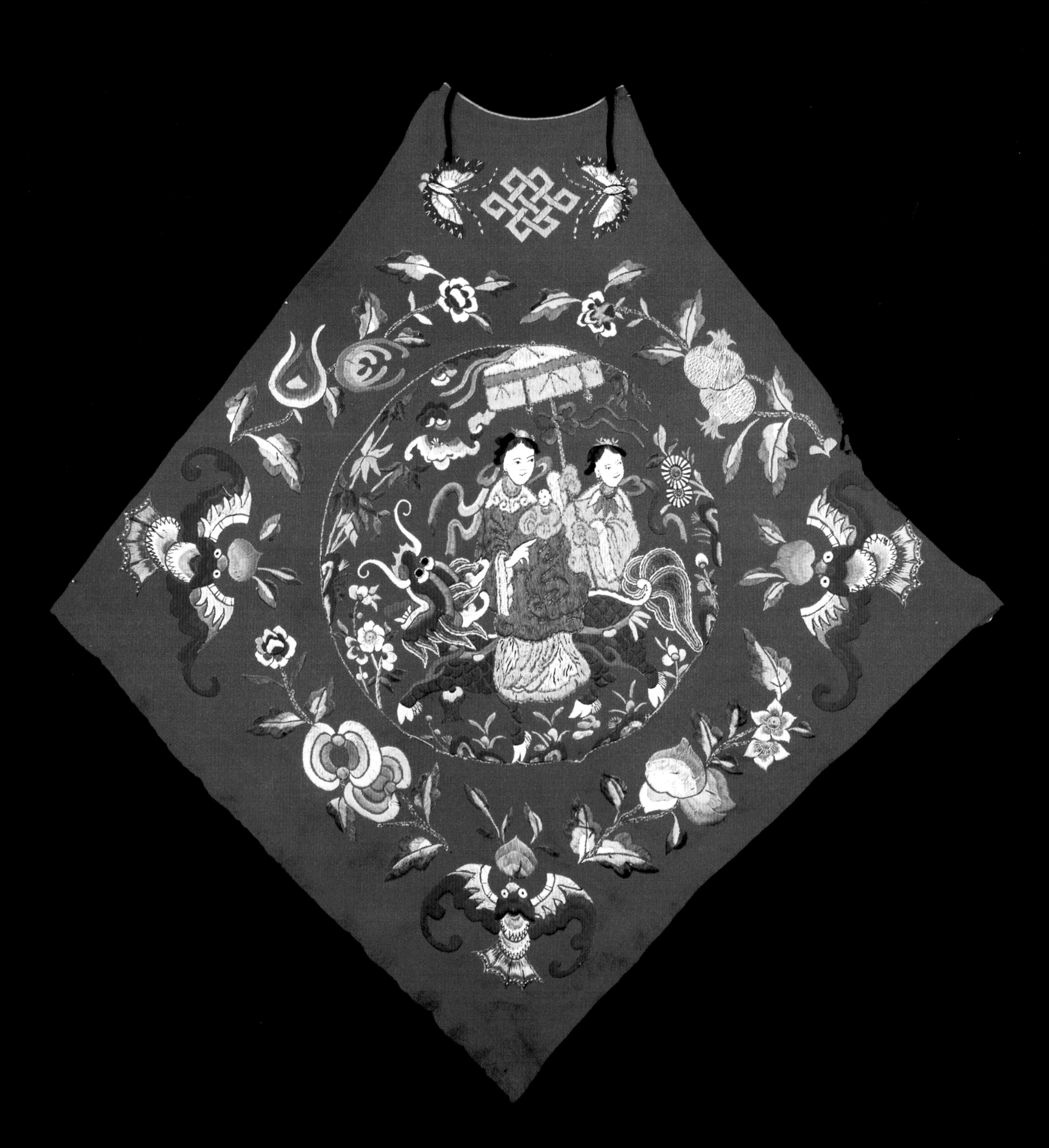

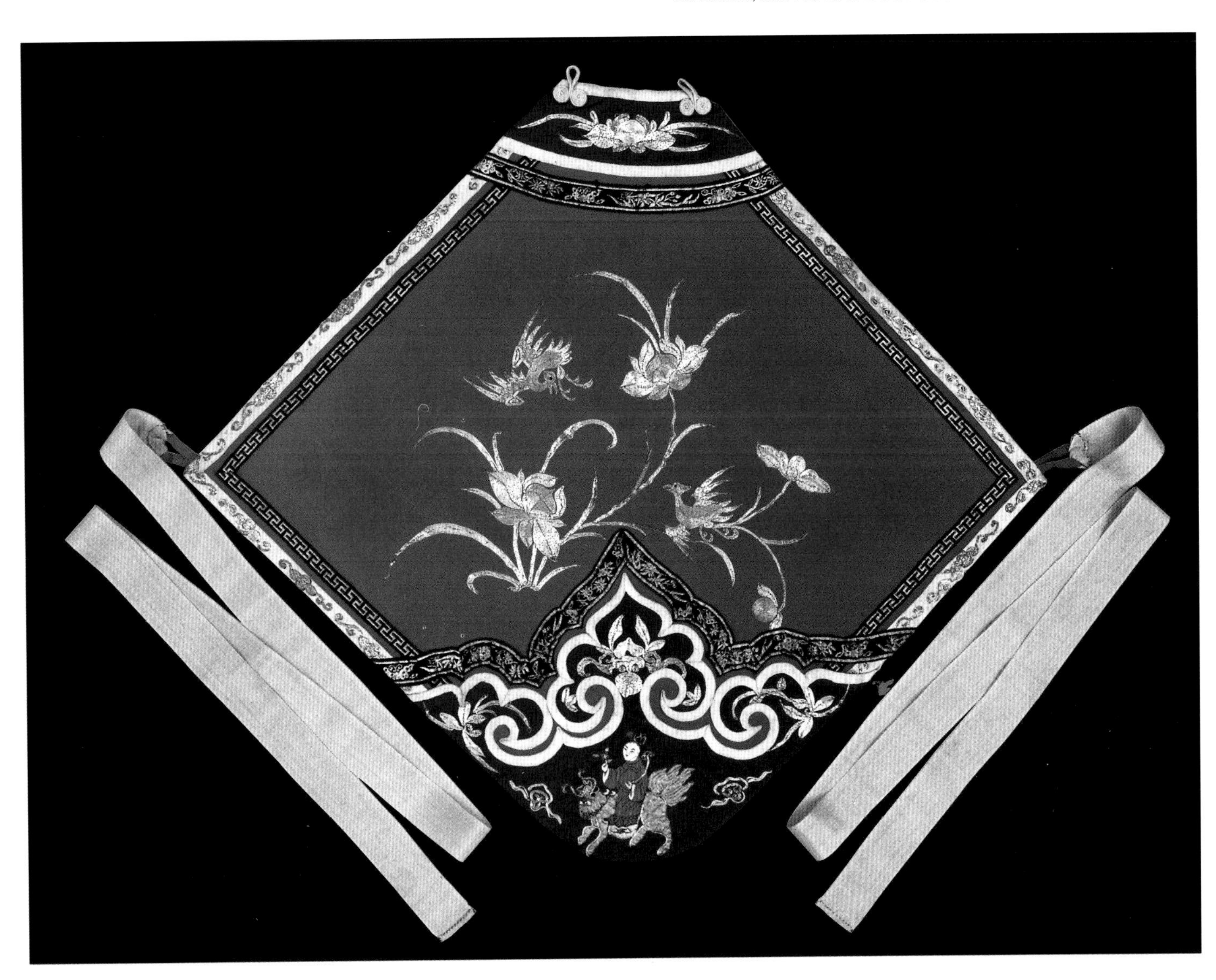

take first place in the imperial examinations. The central motif is surrounded by many other auspicious emblems, such as bats, peaches, pomegranates, Buddha's hand, butterflies, and at the top, the Endless Knot. **Plate 13** shows another in red silk with long tapes to tie at the waist. It is embroidered with couched gold thread in the design of birds and flowers. At the base is the *ruyi* motif in appliqué and a bat, while below that is an embroidered scholar riding on a *qilin* and carrying another *ruyi*.

Often the *doudou* was the only item of clothing worn in the hot summer months until the child was two or three years old. But as long as the garment was embroidered with lucky charms, the mother felt the child was quite safe.

[PLATE 12]

Opposite: Woman's red silk *doudou* with embroidery showing a maiden seated on a *qilin* and carrying a child. Collection of the author.

[PLATE 13]

Above: Woman's red silk *doudou*. Collection of the author.

Plate 14 shows a child's *doudou* made of red silk with a wide opening like a mouth for a pocket. The embroidery in Peking knot is of a padlock, with peach and fish charms, around the child's neck to 'lock him to earth', while below the pocket opening is a scene of a bridge, a phoenix and a *ruyi*. The three *doudou* in **Figure 4** made of resist dye on cotton also have a padlock design; the two outer ones have the god of longevity riding on a *qilin*. These were made in the 1940s and show how some traditions survived well into the twentieth century.

Naval Cover

Infants wore naval covers, and one is seen at the bottom of **Plate 15**. This has the scene in satin stitch on red silk of a scholar returning successfully from an examination. Above it is another type, worn by adults, often referred to as a money belt. This was an elongated oval pouch that fastened with tapes at the back and was worn around the waist and over the stomach to hold daily necessities. The design is of a lotus flower with a cat catching a butterfly.

Endnotes

[1] John Vollmer, *In The Presence of the Dragon Throne*, Royal Ontario Museum, Toronto, Canada, 1977, p. 39.

[2] Schuyler Cammann, *China's Dragon Robes,* Ronald Press, New York, 1952, p. 198.

[3] The collar band is unusual for this period and was possibly added later.

[PLATE 14]

Opposite bottom: Child's *doudou* of red silk, the Peking knot embroidery depicting a padlock and charm necklace, mid-nineteenth century. Collection of the author.

[FIG 4]

Opposite top: Three *doudou* with the designs of padlocks and *qilin* printed with resist dye on cotton, circa 1940.

[PLATE 15]

Right top: Money belt in yellow silk with the design of a cat and a lotus flower. Collection of the author.
Right bottom: Infant's naval cover in red silk with the design of a scholar returning successfully from the examinations. Jobrenco Ltd, Chris Hall Collection Trust.

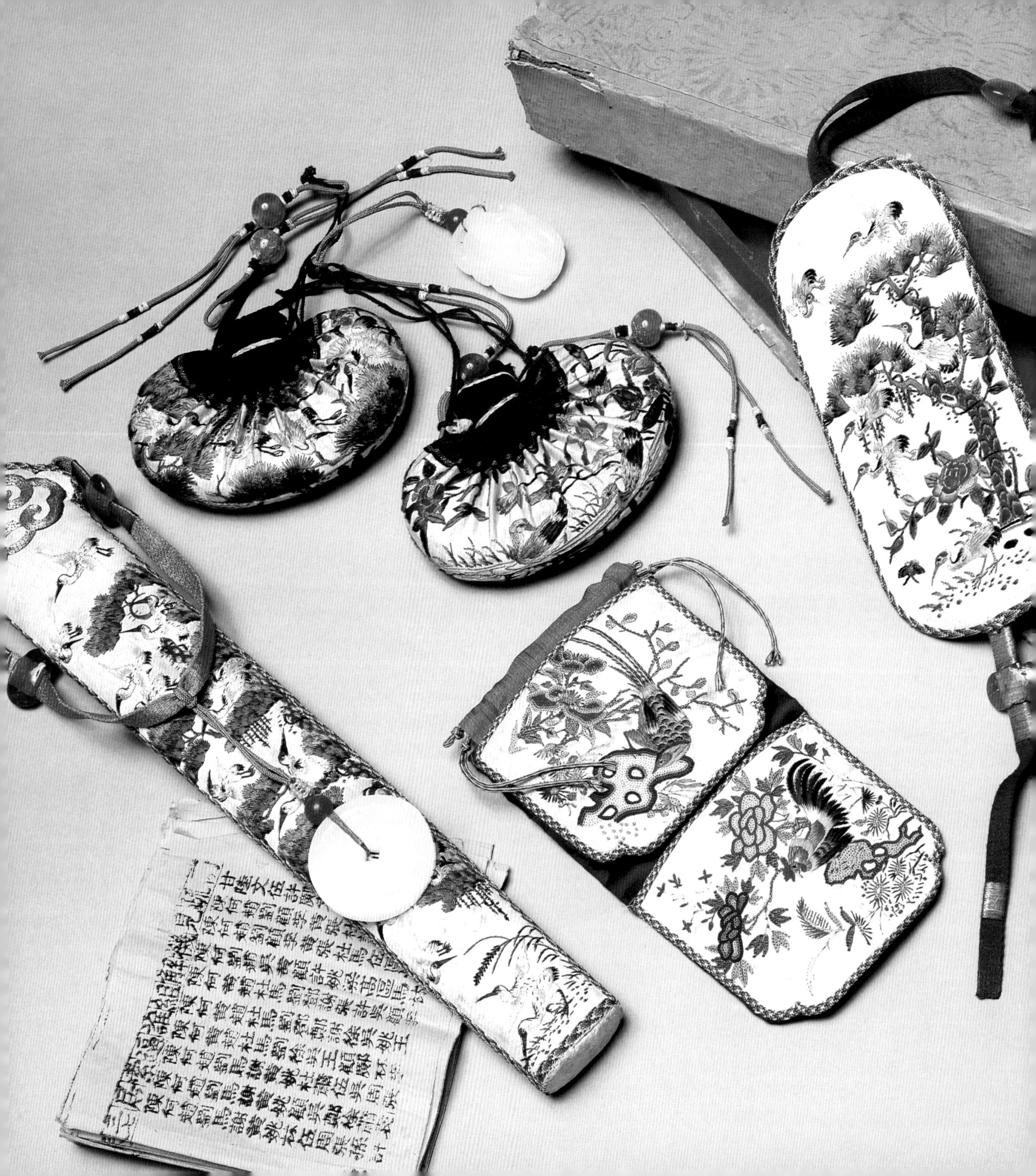

~ *Chapter Six* ~

Purses and Fans

Purses and fans were important accessories during the Qing dynasty and were made in large quantities. From a practical point of view, purses were needed to carry daily necessities, as there were no pockets in gowns or jackets until the beginning of the twentieth century, while the use of a fan to stir the air brought welcome relief in the hot, humid climate. But more than that, as a mark of social standing the type and design of the purse or fan would immediately alert bystanders to the status of the owner.

PURSES

These are still plentiful today, as a purse was a popular and acceptable gift. Certain shops specialised in their manufacture; as with many other trades, there was a street in Beijing devoted to their sale. Women spent many hours producing exquisite purses for their loved ones, and it was the custom for the emperor to reward his courtiers and officials, especially at the Lunar New Year, with purses containing jewelled charms. Purses were given to mark special occasions, and some boxed sets still survive. **Plate 1** shows a set of five purses, still in their original yellow and red paper box, made for presentation to a high official. It contains a fan case and fan, a pair of drawstring purses, a *da lian,* or money purse, and a spectacle case. Embroidered with birds and foliage, the purses have jade counterweights to balance them over the girdle.

"One of the most annoying characteristics of Chinese costume, as seen from the foreign standpoint, is the absence of pockets. . . . If he has a paper of some importance, he carefully unties the strap which confines his trousers to his ankle, inserts the paper, and goes on his way. If he wears outside drawers, he simply tucks in the paper without untying anything. In either case, if the band loosens without his knowledge, the paper is lost—a constant occurrence. Other depositories of such articles are the folds of the long sleeves when turned back, the crown of a turned-up hat, or the space between the cap and the head. Many Chinese make a practice of ensuring a convenient, although somewhat exiguous, supply of ready money, by always sticking a cash in one ear. The main dependence for security of articles carried, is the girdle, to which a small purse, the tobacco pouch and pipe, and similar objects are attached."[1]

Sets of purses had been carried by the Chinese since early times, and the number of items increased as the Qing dynasty drew to a close. The purses shown in Chapter 4, **Plate 6** formed part of the early Qing emperors' set and include a knife case, a compass, and a pair of drawstring purses suspended from the side rings

[PLATE 1]

Opposite: Set of five purses, a fan case, *da lian,* a pair of drawstring purses, and a spectacle case, in their original box. Linda Wrigglesworth, London.

[FIG 1]

The Empress Dowager with her eunuch attendants, wearing purses, including the *da lian,* suspended from their girdles, circa 1903. Her Majesty is carrying a *pien mien* fan.

of the girdle. These purses affirm the nomadic origins of the Manchus, as the drawstring purse would have developed from a circle of leather gathered up to contain pieces of flint needed to strike a flame, fundamental to their way of life.

Later, as the Manchus became settled, the knife case and compass were replaced by items used to suggest the more leisurely and scholarly existence of the Chinese literati. They then included the fan case, *da lian* purse, spectacle case and kerchief holder, though the original drawstring purses were retained. By the end of the nineteenth century, more purses were added, which made it necessary to hang them over the girdle as well as from the rings. These were known as the 'Official Nine', and consisted of most of the following: a pair of drawstring purses, a *da lian* purse, a spectacle case and a fan case, plus a thumb ring box, a tobacco pouch, a watch purse, an oval purse, a holder for brushes and ink and a case for carrying visiting cards. Women, who did not move far from their quarters in the home, simply carried a purse or pendant hung from the top side button on the robe.

The Empress Dowager is seen in **Figure 1** walking to the theatre after her morning audience, accompanied by her attendants and eunuchs; the wife of the Guangxu Emperor is on her right. The tightly girdled dragon robes worn by the eunuchs have *da lian* purses hanging from their girdles. **Plate 2** shows an uncut set of six cases: from the top are a kerchief holder, two drawstring purses, a fan case, a *da lian* purse and a spectacle case. They are embroidered on silk gauze with a geometric design.

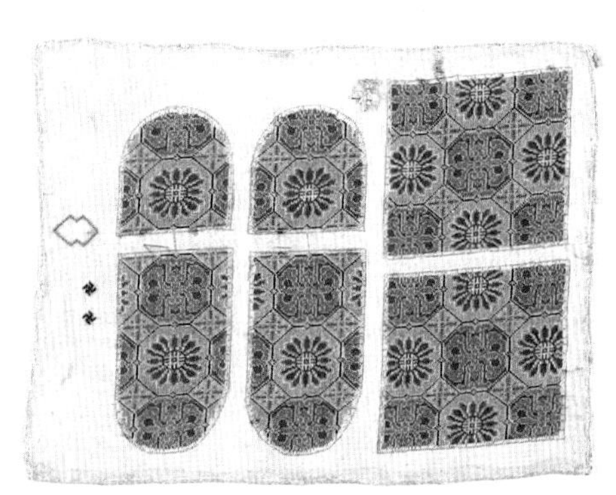

[PLATE 2]
Set of six uncut cases in counted stitch on silk gauze: a kerchief holder, two drawstring purses, a fan case, a *da lian* purse and a spectacle case. Linda Wrigglesworth, London.

Drawstring Purse

The most important of all were the drawstring or heartshaped purses, due to their origins as leather pouches for flint. In the Regulations these were shown in pairs and hung from the girdle rings at each side of the robe. Once established in China, the Manchu emperors kept areca (betel) nuts in them. The Qianlong Emperor "took from his girdle . . . a plain yellow silk [purse] with the figure of the five-clawed dragon, and some Tartar characters worked into it" and presented it to young George Staunton, who accompanied his father and Lord Macartney on the embassy to China from 1792–94.[2] Other uses were to hold scented cotton or aromatic herbs to sweeten the sometimes putrid air.

The lower part of the drawstring purse was densely embroidered, often in Peking knot or tent stitch, while the top part was finely pleated. A cord was attached to suspend the purses from the girdle. Two knotted strings ending in long tassels hung from each side. The pair of purses shown in **Plate 3** date from the mid-nineteenth century and have the Four Treasures and some ritual vessels embroidered on both sides in tent stitch on silk gauze.

Fan Case

Folding fans were carried in narrow tapering cases suspended by a cord from the girdle. These cases were elaborately embroidered in silk, often with characters recording the occasion on which they were presented. The fan case in **Plate 3** matches the drawstring purses, while the fan case in **Plate 4** is in yellow silk with an embroidered design of a cockerel among vines and flowers. Another, in **Plate 5**, is of eight horses, four on each side, in padded Pekinese stitch.

Da lian Purse

The *da lian* was a flat rectangular purse used to carry money. The two end flap pockets were reinforced with card and embroidered, and there was a hidden inside pocket in the soft silk. At first it was suspended by a cord from the girdle, but later one of the flaps hung over the girdle. The one featured in **Plate 6** is in cream and blue silk embroidered with butterflies and bats.

[PLATE 3]

Opposite: Pair of drawstring purses embroidered in tent stitch and a matching fan case, all embroidered with the Four Attributes. Collection of the author.

[PLATE 6]

Below: *Da lian* purse in cream and blue silk embroidered with a design of butterflies and bats. Collection of the author.

[PLATE 4]

Opposite right: Fan case embroidered on yellow silk with a cockerel among vines and flowers. Collection of the author.

[PLATE 5]

Opposite left: Fan case with horses embroidered in padded Pekinese stitch. Collection of the author.

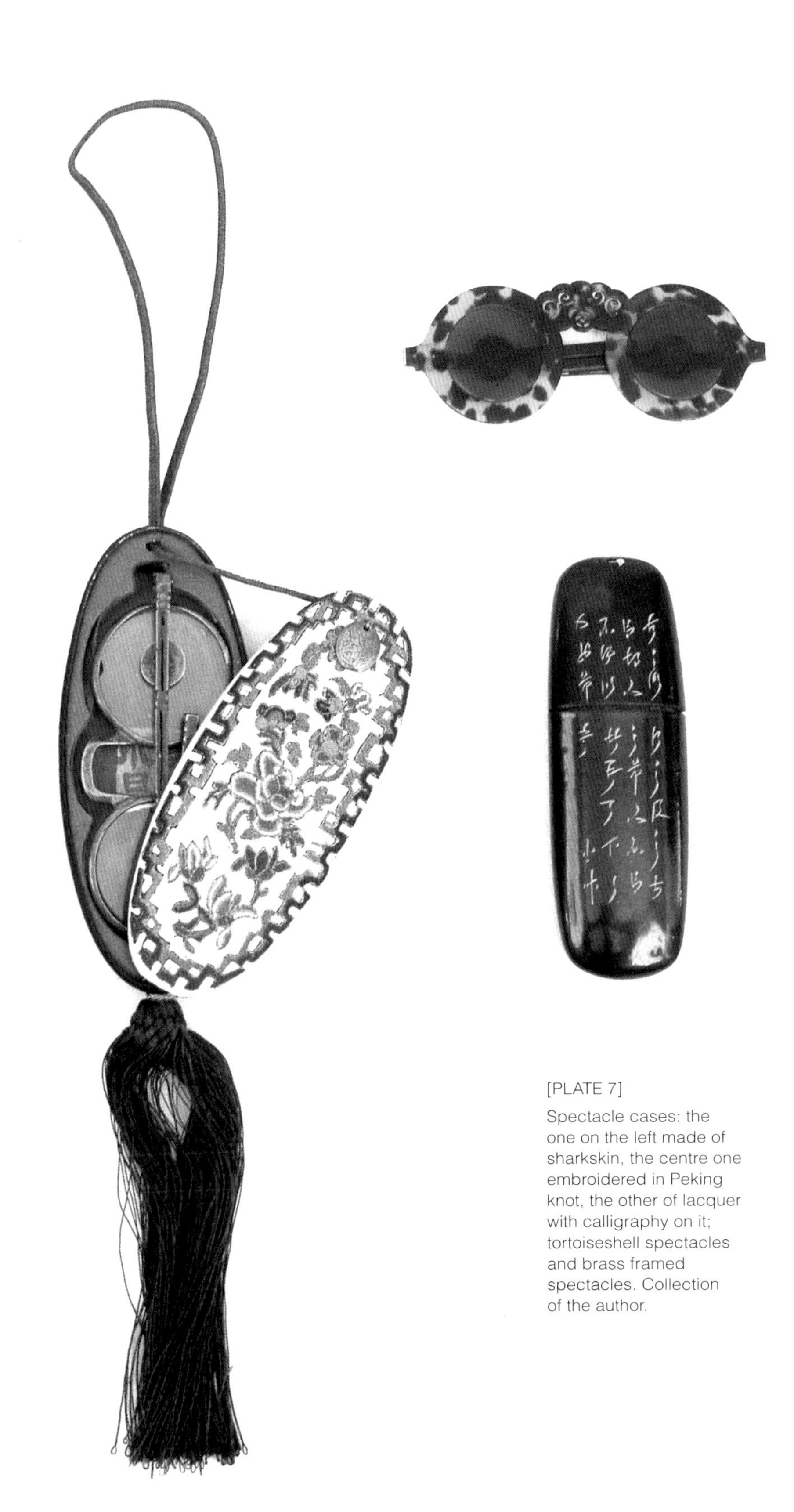

[PLATE 7]

Spectacle cases: the one on the left made of sharkskin, the centre one embroidered in Peking knot, the other of lacquer with calligraphy on it; tortoiseshell spectacles and brass framed spectacles. Collection of the author.

Spectacle Case

The Chinese had made use of magnifying glasses placed in frames as early as possibly the tenth century, but it was not until the nineteenth century that cylindrical lens were worn. They were made from crystal, smoky quartz and a type of rose quartz, ground away until the prescription was met. "When worn, the rim rests upon the cheek-bones; the frame has a hinge between the glasses, and the machine is sometimes kept on the ears by loops or weights. Foreign-shaped spectacles are supplanting these primitive optics, but the prejudice is still in favour of crystal."[3]

Reginald Johnston, tutor to the deposed Xuantong Emperor writes of the difficulty in 1921 of having spectacles prescribed for the emperor, being informed that "the wearing of spectacles by emperors is a thing that is not done."[4] However, not all were so hidebound by tradition, and the use of spectacles was seen as an indication of wealth and learning, as only those rich enough could afford them.

The spectacles and cases shown in **Plate 7** date from the late nineteenth to early twentieth centuries. The case on the left is made of sharkskin (shagreen) trimmed with brass, while the one on the right is of lacquer with calligraphy on it. At the top, the pair of spectacles made of tortoiseshell have tinted lenses for bright sunlight. The spectacles in the centre have brass frames with magnifying lenses. Their accompanying case has Peking knot embroidery in a flower design, and the label inside states that the spectacle lenses are made of real crystal.

Kerchief Holder

Kerchief holders were attached to the side top button on a woman's garment or looped and weighted over the man's girdle. The kerchiefs were plain, coloured silk squares which tucked into openings on each side of the holder at the top. In **Plate 8** the group of purses for a man, that includes a fan case, a drawstring purse (the other possibly missing), a spectacle case, and a kerchief holder, are all made of ochre yellow silk with bats embroidered in Peking knot in the three shades of blue.

Tobacco Pouch

Tobacco was smoked by both men and women, as it was thought to have medicinal properties. Gourd-shaped purses were filled with tobacco, opening at one side only so that the long-stemmed pipe could be inserted. They were often suspended by a cord from the stem of the pipe. The one in **Plate 9** is embroidered with Pekinese stitch on blue-black silk. On one side is a phoenix and a deer, while on the reverse are fish and coins. In **Plate 10** a detail of a painting from the mid-nineteenth century shows a lady, with a long-stemmed pipe and a tobacco pouch hanging from it, being offered a selection of purses by a hawker.

Plate 11 shows four purses made for ladies in the early twentieth century in Shanghai. The pair of tobacco pouches in voided satin stitch have a geometric design on one side and a floral one on the reverse, with decorative tassels at each side. The fan case and matching spectacle case are in cream silk with pink silk on the reverse and edged with gold couching.

[PLATE 8]

Opposite: A group of purses for a man, including a kerchief holder embroidered in Peking knot. Collection of the author.

[PLATE 9]

Below: Gourd-shaped tobacco pouch with a phoenix and a deer embroidered in Pekinese stitch. Collection of the author.

[PLATE 10]

Opposite: A lady with a long-stemmed pipe and a tobacco pouch hanging from it being offered a selection of purses by a hawker, circa 1850.

[PLATE 11]

Below: A lady's fan case, a matching spectacle case and a pair of tobacco pouches, made in Shanghai, early twentieth century. Collection of the author.

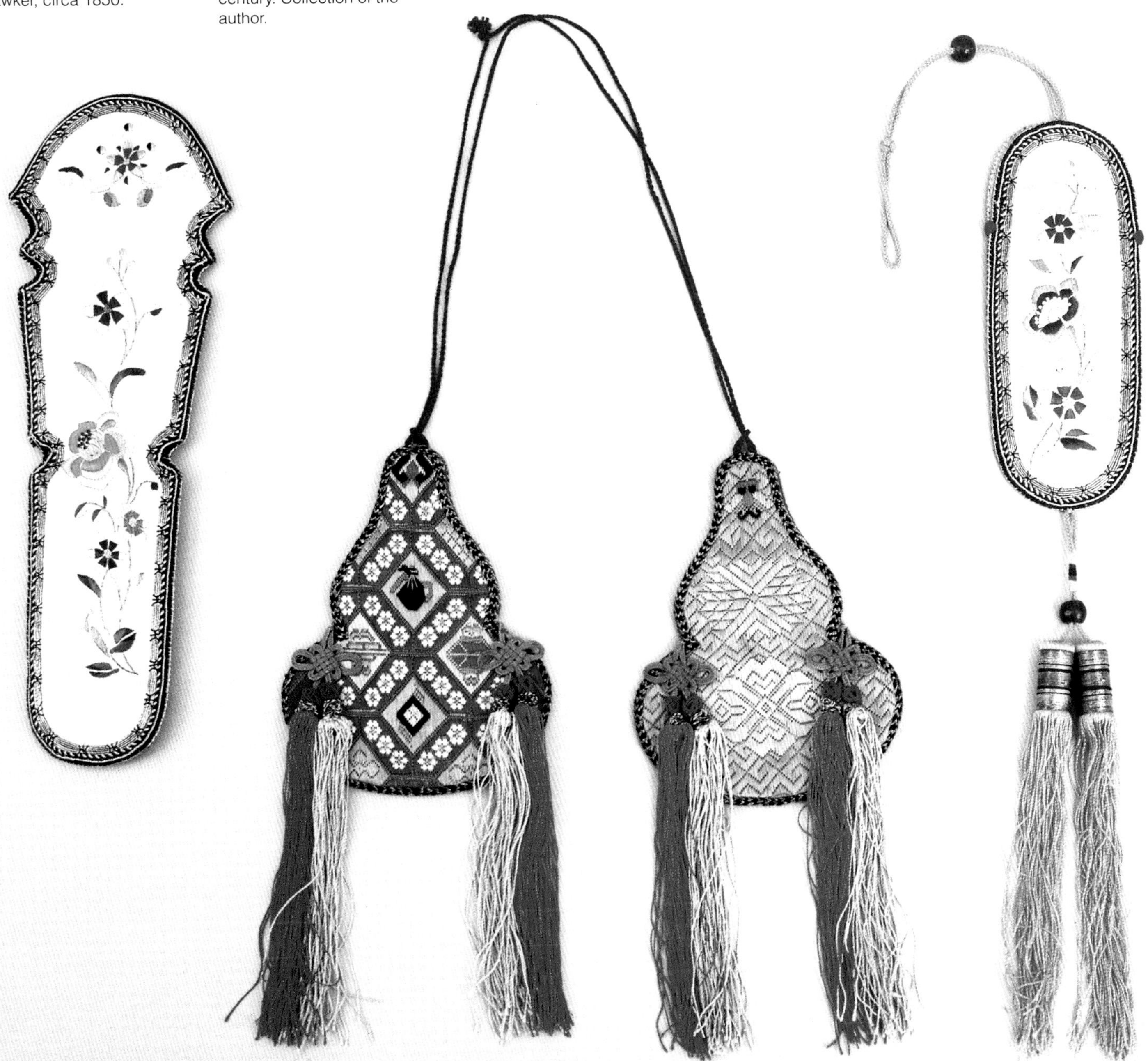

[PLATE 12]

Left and centre: One of a pair of jade thumb rings and its case decorated with appliquéd peonies on red silk. Collection of the author. Right: Seal box in yellow silk with characters in black ink stating that the owner has gained first place in the examinations. Don J. Cohn.

[PLATE 13]

Opposite: Oval purse with a scene of a river and figures, *da lian* purse for a pocket watch, and fan case. Collection of the author.

Thumb Ring Case

Plate 12 shows a case in red silk, with peonies painted and appliquéd in silk, made to contain a pair of thumb rings, like the jade one shown here. As mentioned in Chapter 4, a thumb ring was worn originally by military officials when pulling the bow, but they were later adopted by the literati, who wore one on each thumb.

Seal Box

Seals or chops were carried and used as personal signatures, as well as signs of possession, in a country where many people were illiterate and unable to write their name. Seals were carved from a variety of materials, such as jade, ivory and soapstone. Little boxes were made to contain the seal, as seen on the right in **Plate 12**. This one, in yellow silk, has a red silk cross with characters in black ink hyperbolically stating that the owner has gained first place in the examinations. The yellow silk and the shape of the box are a miniature version of imperial seals, and it would have been presented as a symbolic gesture.

Oval Purse

The oval purse was often only embroidered on the lower half of the front, as the upper portion was frequently pleated to hang from the girdle. The front was stiffened with card, while the back was always of plain cotton. There were several inside compartments to carry such things as pieces of fingering jade. The purse in **Plate 13** has a river scene embroidered in Pekinese stitch, with a serving maid greeting a scholar sitting in

[PLATE 14]
Left: Square purse with the design of a student kneeling at the feet of his instructor. Collection of the author. Right: Square purse in green silk with the Four Attributes in Pekinese stitch. Collection of the author. Centre: Purse in Peking knot of a lady looking over a wall. Jobrenco Ltd, Chris Hall Collection Trust.

a sampan surrounded by cypress trees, willow trees and sacred fungus.

Watch Purse

Having a pocket watch was a sign of wealth, and was flaunted by those who could afford to carry one. The watch purse shown above the oval purse in **Plate 13** is in the same style as the *da lian* purse and shows a golden pheasant amid peonies and sacred fungus embroidered in Pekinese and long-and-short stitch, while around the open face of the watch pocket are more flowers. Also in **Plate 13** is the reverse side of the fan case shown in **Plate 4**, showing the peacock amid flowers.

Square Purse

This purse type is suspended by a cord with a tassel which passes through and over the girdle. The simplest kind was made of two embroidered squares joined on three sides. The one on the left in **Plate 14** has a design in Pekinese stitch of a student kneeling at the feet of his instructor. The type on the right has pockets in the centre, front and back, all stiffened with card. This one is in green silk and depicts two of the Four Attributes of the Scholar embroidered in Pekinese stitch. Another kind, worn flat against the body, has a folded piece, often in plain cotton, at the top through which the girdle would pass. The one in the centre of **Plate 14** has Peking knot embroidery of a lady wistfully leaning over the wall of her compound while outside more women take a stroll.

Brush and Pen Purse

Calligraphy and painting were two of the gentlemanly accomplishments, and Chinese men needed a purse to carry their bamboo-handled brushes and sticks of solid ink, which were ground with water to produce ink. The purse for brushes in **Plate 15** is embroidered in Peking knot with a design of peonies, vases, *ruyi,* and ritual vessels. The one on the right resembles a fan holder but has a cord which passes through the

[PLATE 15]
Paintbrush holder embroidered in Peking knot with a design of peonies, vase and books; another brush holder in black satin. Collection of the author.

[PLATE 16]

Right: Bell-shaped key holder in Peking knot and satin stitch. Collection of the author. Left: Rectangular key holder with a design of peonies in Peking knot. Jobrenco Ltd, Chris Hall Collection Trust.

[PLATE 17]

Opposite: Visiting card case in black satin embroidered with couched gold and silver thread. Collection of the author. Another with the design of a bat in counted stitch. Jobrenco Ltd, Chris Hall Collection Trust.

centre to make divisions for the brushes. It is made of black satin reversing to blue; the very poetic embroidered inscription states its purpose.

Key Holder

Key holders were suspended from a cord through which the key was attached and hidden inside the holder. **Plate 16** shows a key holder shaped like a bell with the opening at the bottom, decorated with a design in Peking knot and satin stitch of a successful scholar shielded by a servant carrying an umbrella. Only persons of high rank were entitled to have an official umbrella. The second one is rectangular in shape with peonies embroidered entirely in Peking knot.

Visiting Card Holder

Visiting cards were carried in rectangular holders with a pullout drawer like those shown in **Plate 17**. The first is made of black silk on stiff card embroidered with couched gold thread in a design of ritual vessels, while the other is of counted stitch on silk gauze over a card base with the design of a bat against a key fret background.

Letter Case

A letter case was used to hold letters or small documents. Normally folded vertically into three, they were carried by men who tucked them down the side of their knee-high boots. The outside was plain, of silk or sometimes leather, but the many pockets inside were richly embroidered with couplets and proverbs, as well as auspicious symbols of flowers and birds. The one in **Plate 18** has a design of a peacock in a garden on the central

compartment. The poetic calligraphy on the left is in harmony with the embroidery design, while the panel on the right shows two lions at play.

Snuff Bottle Purse

Made from ground tobacco spiced with aromatic herbs, snuff was introduced to China by Europeans during the Ming dynasty as a remedy for nasal congestion. But because the Chinese literati grew their fingernails long, it was not easy for them to take snuff from boxes, as was the custom in the west. Moreover, the humid climate, especially in the south, meant that snuff kept in boxes deteriorated quickly. Therefore tiny bottles, less than 8 centimetres high, with a narrow neck were used to hold the snuff. Each had a small spoon fixed to the stopper. The snuff was transferred with the spoon to the back of the left thumb and then inhaled. The small bottles were easy to carry, either tucked into the sleeves or suspended in a small purse such as this one. The little box in **Plate 19**, made of red silk over stiffened card, has a design in raised Peking knot of a crane in a garden.

Lishi Holder

Brides at weddings carried a *lishi* holder suspended from a cord around the neck to hold all the money given to the new couple. The one on the left in **Plate 20** has two dragons above a sea wave border and mountain, while the characters in the centre stand for 'everything good you wish yourself'.

[PLATE 18]

Opposite top: Letter case in three sections with an embroidered design of birds, lions and calligraphy. Don J. Cohn.

[PLATE 19]

Right: Snuff bottle holder in red silk with a design in raised Peking knot of a crane in a garden. Collection of the author.

[PLATE 20]

Opposite bottom: *Li shi* holder with an inscription, the characters stating "everything good you wish yourself." Collection of the author. Folding money purse with two horizontal pockets. Twentieth century. Don J. Cohn.

Money Purse

This type had two or three horizontal pouches for money which could be folded up and carried in the hand or hung from a top loop. Seen here in **Plate 20**, the purse is embroidered in satin stitch in a design of lotus flowers, peaches and pomegranates.

FANS

Fans were an important accessory for the Chinese for thousands of years. The earliest, recorded as far back as the Shang dynasty (circa 1600–1100 B.C.), were made of pheasant or peacock feathers. Rigid round or oval fans, called *pien mien,* were popular in the Tang dynasty (A.D. 618–906). They were made of bamboo or ivory with silk stretched across the frame and embroidered or painted. The one in **Plate 21**, dating to the nineteenth century, is made of silk stretched across a wooden frame. The embroidered design is of two cranes surrounded by bamboo and flowers. This type continued to be carried until the end of the nineteenth century, as seen here in **Figure 2**, where three young Chinese girls are holding circular *pien mien*.

During the Song dynasty folding fans made of horn, bone, ivory and sandalwood were introduced into China from Japan via Korea, and by the early fifteenth century they had become very fashionable because of their convenience. The number of ribs varied from around ten to thirty. A wealthy man would carry his fan in a case attached to his girdle or tucked into the top of his boots, while a coolie would keep it in his stocking top, or down the back of the neck of his jacket.[5] A fan was also used to gesticulate and make a point. The literati used them as a means of artistic expression, having them inscribed with calligraphy and paintings. Many famous Chinese artists painted landscapes, flowers, birds or insects on paper to be made into fans. **Figure 3** shows a scholar holding a folding painted paper fan.

Paper fans had sticks made of thin slivers of bamboo or, to sweeten the air, scented woods such as camphor, cedar or sandalwood. On the right of **Plate 22** is a man's paper folding fan which has thirty bamboo sticks with a woodcut atlas and flags on the leaf. In the centre is a sandalwood and feather fan with twenty pierced sticks with a decorative pattern. The label on the box says it came from Cheong Kee Sang, dealer in Canton (Guangzhou) of "Folding fans of Sandal Wood Ivory bone Lacquered Gilt embroidered painted with pictures of the Fans of Silk and Feather of the best quality Price Moderate." On the left is a tortoiseshell brise fan with twenty-one sticks, made for an official. According to the tiny engraved inscription, it was presented "from your humble concubine with best wishes" to her husband Mou Jia Wei, in the thirtieth year of the reign of Guangxu (1904). Four larger characters denote "In the quiet of the hermitage, one feels pure pleasure."

Rigid feather fans in an elongated oval were popular at the end of the nineteenth century, and some older men still carry them today. The man's fan on the right in **Plate 23** is of twelve feathers inserted in an ivory handle; the woman's fan on the left features twenty-six egret feathers with a silk rosette at the ivory handle.

[PLATE 21]

Opposite: *Pien mien* fan of cranes and bamboo embroidered on silk in a wooden frame, nineteenth century. Teresa Coleman Fine Arts, Hong Kong.

[FIG 2]

Above: Chinese women holding *pien mien* fans.

[FIG 3]

Left: A scholar holding a paper folding fan.

[PLATE 22]

Men's folding fans: one of tortoiseshell, one of sandalwood and feathers, the third of paper and bamboo sticks with a woodblock print of an atlas and flags. Collection of the author.

Endnotes

[1] Arthur H. Smith, *Chinese Characteristics*, pub. Fleming H. Revell Company, New York, 1894, p. 128.

[2] Sir George Staunton, *An Authentic Account of An Embassy from The King of Great Britain to the Emperor of China*, London, 1797, vol. 2, p. 235.

[3] S. Wells Williams, *The Middle Kingdom*, 1895, reprinted Paragon Book Reprint Corp., New York, 1966, vol. 2, p. 22.

[4] Reginald F. Johnston, *Twilight in the Forbidden City*, Victor Gollancz Ltd, 1934, reprinted Oxford University Press, Hong Kong, 1985, p. 272.

[5] Other types of folding fan were made in Guangzhou during the eighteenth and nineteenth centuries solely for export to the west. Most were brise fans made of bone, ivory or mother of pearl, but paper fans, so-called 'mandarin fans', were also popular. These had figures of mandarins dressed in tiny scraps of silk with painted ivory faces.

[PLATE 23]

Rigid feather fans, the lady's fan (on the left) made of goose feathers with a silk rosette, the man's fan (on the right) made of feathers inserted into an ivory handle. Collection of the author.

~ *Chapter Seven* ~

Footwear

Footwear was not specified in the *Huangchao liqi tushi*, but as will be shown, the types worn distinguished the different classes of society. All styles of boots and shoes could fit either foot, with only a cursory attempt to follow the outline of the natural foot. Even more uncomfortable was the fashion among Han Chinese women for binding their feet to make them very small. This suffering was imposed to imply status; only the poorest people went barefoot.

MEN'S FOOTWEAR

Boots

The possession of boots was seen as a demonstration of wealth and superiority, and they could only be worn by officials and men with some position in society. A proverb of the day stated: "A man in boots will not speak to a man in shoes."[1]

To match his yellow silk court robes, the emperor wore yellow silk brocade boots. Those seen in **Figure 1**, said to have belonged to the Kangxi Emperor, are decorated at the cuff and on the vamp with black brocade trimmed with rows of seed pearls and coral beads. The thick soles would have been made of layers of felted paper with a final layer of leather, and whitened around the edges. A loop at the top of the boot allowed a garter to be passed through to prevent the boot from slipping down the leg. Inner socks can be seen emerging from the top of the boots.

Plain black satin knee-high boots were worn by the emperor for informal wear, and by princes, noblemen and mandarins for general use. **Figure 2** shows a photo taken around 1880 of an imperial prince wearing a pair of black satin boots. Similar boots in **Figure 3** were made for a mandarin and have leather piping reinforcing the front and back seams, with 7 centimetre thick

[PLATE 2]

Opposite: Men's shoes with contrast appliqué designs. Collection of the author.

[FIG 1]

Left: The Kangxi Emperor's yellow silk brocade boots, decorated with bands of black brocade and rows of seed pearls and coral beads. Palace Museum, Beijing.

[FIG 2]

Right: An imperial prince, wearing a pair of black satin boots, with two of his children, the one standing wearing shoes resembling an animal, circa 1880.

[FIG 3]

Opposite, top: Pair of black satin boots belonging to an official. Collection of the author.

[FIG 4]

Opposite, bottom: Men's socks, one pair in white cotton and the other in blue silk, both with cotton soles. Collection of the author.

white soles. These inflexible soles originally allowed the Manchus to stand in the stirrups when riding horseback, and were made shorter than the vamp at the toe to make them easier to walk in, although the implication of wearing such boots was that the mandarin never travelled anywhere on foot.

More flexible, shorter boots in black velvet or satin with thin leather or cotton soles were worn by lower ranks such as military troops, clerks and attendants. **Plate 1** shows a pair of black velvet boots trimmed at the cuff with satin. The pair of blue quilted cotton covers button neatly over the boots for protection when not being worn. Boots were expensive: a pair with high white soles could cost as much as a servant's wages for the year.[2]

Shoes

Shoes were used by the gentry for informal wear within the private quarters of the home and for common use by the lower ranks. Like the boots, some shoes had a stiff sole several centimetres thick, made of layers of paper, to raise the vamp and keep it dryer in wet weather. There were two main styles for men, one with a rounded toe curving back to the sole, and the other with a wide toe the same width as the heel. Again, like the boots, the inflexible sole was made shorter than the uppers in order to give sufficient spring for walking.

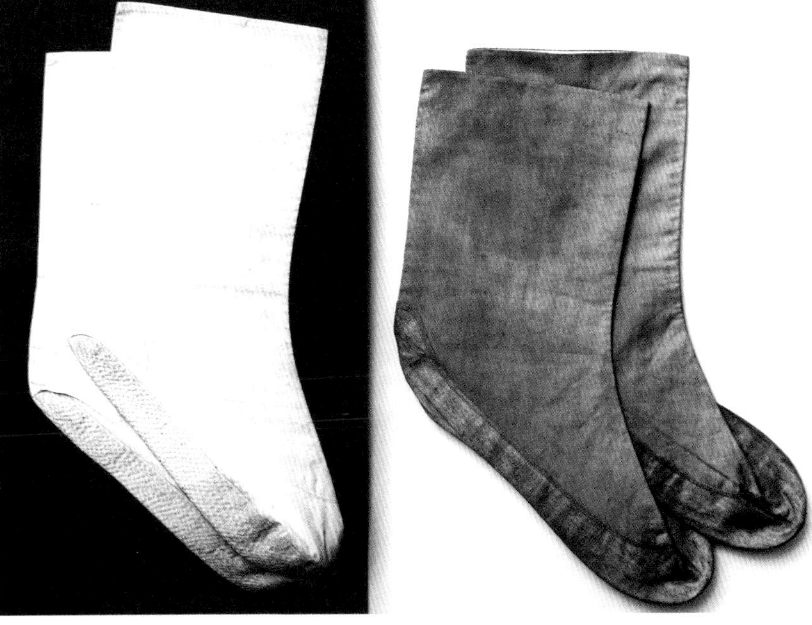

The vamps on the shoes were of black satin, cotton or velvet, plain or appliquéd; leather was used only for the trimming or binding. In **Plate 2** the pair of shoes on the right has an appliquéd

design of clouds in black velvet on beige silk, while the other pair are of blue satin trimmed with black satin, with the *shou* character on the toe. A backless mule in the same shape as the satin shoe was worn for summer, or as slippers, made of woven straw or cane for the vamp. The soles were also made of straw, or else had padded cotton or silk with a leather sole, like those illustrated in **Plate 3**.

Socks, Puttees and Knee Pads

Socks were worn inside the boots, as can be seen in the emperor's boots in **Figure 1**. Those worn in the cooler months were made of silk, cotton or linen, lined and padded with rows of stitching; they were knee length, and opened down the back, with a vamp but no sole. Another type of sock for warmer weather was shorter, embroidered or plain in blue or white silk or cotton. They were worn with shoes and pulled over the hem of the trousers. The pair on the left in **Figure 4** are in white cotton, while those on the right are in blue silk lined with white cotton; both pairs have reinforced stitching along the cotton soles and heels.

Lengths of tightly woven silk about 8 centimetres wide and 85 to 120 centimetres long, often with silken fringes at each end, were used as puttees and wound spirally around the leg from ankle to knee, over the trousers and socks, for protection and support. Those in **Plate 4** have a damask design at the ends. Also in **Plate 4** is a pair of embroidered knee pads in black silk thickly padded and lined with blue silk, with ties to fasten around the knee. They were useful for cushioning the knees when required to perform the full *kowtow*.[3] A pair of narrow trouser garters with gold couched embroidery of classical emblems such as the *ruyi* have blue silk ties that could have been threaded through the loops on the top of the boots, as seen in **Figure 1**, or else used to hold up the trousers at the knee.

WOMEN'S FOOTWEAR

Manchu Women's Shoes

The womenfolk of the ruling Manchus did not bind their feet; instead those in high-ranking families wore a special shoe, exaggeratedly elevated, with a concave heel in the centre of the instep. As well as imitating the swaying gait caused by bound feet, it also made them tower over the diminutive Chinese: ". . . the shoes stand upon a sole of four or six inches [10–15 centimetres] in height, or even more. These soles, which consist of a wooden frame upon which white cotton cloth is stretched, are quite thin from the toe and heel to about the centre of the foot, when they curve abruptly downwards, forming a base of two or three inches square

[PLATE 1]

Opposite, top: Blue quilted cotton protectors for boots; short black velvet boots. Collection of the author.

[Plate 3]

Opposite, bottom: Man's slippers made of woven rushes with a blue silk inner lining. Collection of the author.

[PLATE 4]

Left: Knee pads in black silk; trouser garters in cream silk; a pair of black woven silk puttees. Collection of the author.

[5–8 centimetres]. In use they are exceedingly inconvenient, but . . . they show the well-to-do position of the wearer. The Manchus are . . . a taller . . . race than the Chinese, and the artificial increase to the height afforded by these shoes gives them at times almost startling proportions."[4]

The bottom of the shoe was padded with layers of cotton to prevent jarring when walking. The vamp was made of silk and embroidered with designs of flowers, birds and fruit. The pair shown in **Plate 5** have a red satin vamp with flowers embroidered in shades of blue, and cotton-covered soles, the seams and edges outlined with black satin. **Plate 6** shows a pattern for a pair of Manchu ladies' shoes, with the central insert and a heel flap. The yellow silk background and the finely detailed design in *kesi* of phoenixes and peonies suggests the shoes were intended for a lady at court.

Photographs of Manchu noblewomen usually show the robe reaching to the ground and concealing the heel, but ones taken of the Empress Dowager Cixi frequently show the hem of her robe deliberately raised a little at the ankle to reveal a splendidly decorated shoe. In **Figure 5** she is seen with ladies of her court in a photograph taken in 1903. Although she was by

[PLATE 5]

Opposite: Manchu women's shoes with a satin vamp embroidered with flowers and cotton-covered soles. Collection of the author.

[PLATE 6]

Above: Patterns for a pair of Manchu ladies' shoes, with a finely detailed design in *kesi* of phoenixes and peonies. Jobrenco Ltd, Chris Hall Collection Trust.

[FIG 5]
Empress Dowager Cixi with her ladies-in-waiting, 1903. The Empress Dowager displays elevated shoes dripping with strings of pearls.

that date sixty-eight years of age, she retained her keen love of dress, and the heels of her elevated shoes are dripping with strings of pearls which match her splendid pearl collar.

The shoes with concave heels must have been quite difficult to walk in, and for informal wear, as well as among the lower ranks of Manchu women, shoes with boat-shaped convex soles were worn. The two pairs seen in **Plate 7** have thick soles made of layers of paper above a layer of leather. The vamp of one is in appliquéd silk, the other densely embroidered with a flower design. At other informal occasions, women wore shoes similar to the men's shoes in **Plate 2**.

Bound Feet Shoes

The Han Chinese tradition of binding women's feet to make them appear as small as a lotus bud was thought to have started between the end of the Tang dynasty and the beginning of the Song. Legend has it that a favourite consort of the emperor, while dancing, bound her feet to represent a new moon. The style was quickly taken up by the women at court, and gradually spread outside court circles until it was almost universal in China. The smell and size of the small foot, together with the woman's teetering gait, produced erotic associations for men, and few mothers would risk their daughters being

[PLATE 7]
Manchu informal shoes with boat-shaped thick soles. Collection of the author.

unable to marry if allowed to have natural feet.

The Manchus, on taking power, tried unsuccessfully to ban the custom, and most Chinese women continued to bow to pressure and bind their daughters' feet. It was not until the end of the nineteenth century that footbinding started to decline. Various anti-footbinding societies were formed by westerners to promote its demise. Mrs. Archibald Little, the wife of a Yangzi River merchant and scholar, was a leading exponent of the Natural Feet Society and very active in the fight at the turn of the century to denounce footbinding. It was banned by the new Republic in 1912, and gradually died out, although there was resistance to having natural feet in much of the country for some decades after that.

Footbinding began any time when the girl was between three and twelve years of age. A binding cloth about 10 centimetres wide and around 250 centimetres long, of woven silk or cotton, either natural or dyed indigo blue, was tightly wrapped around the foot, starting at the toes, which were forced in towards the sole. The bandage wrapped around the heel to further force the toes and heel in towards each other.

The binding custom varied from region to region. Sometimes a wet cloth was used so that

as it dried it tightened to give greater support; at other times a small block of wood was inserted under the heel for support and the bandages wrapped over. Women sat on a special binding stool which held the bandages attached to a roller. As the handle turned, the bandages tightened, which helped to deaden the pain. Following a visit to Shantou (Swatow), a treaty port in Guangdong province, Mrs. Little wrote that girls' feet were not bound until they were almost thirteen so they could do more work, at which time "the foot is already too much formed for it to be possible to do more than narrow it by binding all the toes but the big one underneath the foot. An abnormally high heel is however worn, and this gives to the foot, placed slanting upon it, the appearance of being short. There is often a little round hole at the tip of the shoe through which the great toe can be seen."[5] This style can be seen in **Plate 10**, in black cotton with open toes. This type of binding was easier to unbind, and Mrs. Little reported instances of the foot being unbound when the woman was in her early twenties and returning to its natural size in a few years.[6]

The feet were usually bound to a length of 13 centimetres; the 3-inch (7-centimetre) lotus was quite rare, and only for women who had servants to support them while walking. In some cases the woman was carried on the servant's back. "The appearance of the deformed member when uncovered is shocking, crushed out of all proportion and beauty, and covered with a wrinkled and lifeless skin like that of a washwoman's hands daily immersed in soapsuds."[7]

As part of her dowry, a woman would make several pairs of shoes, proof of her needlework ability as well as her small feet. First the vamp was made, of silk or cotton and embroidered, then the heel and sole which were made of densely layered and stitched white cotton; finally the vamp was joined to the sole.[8] A heel tongue and loops at the sides enabled the shoes to be pulled onto the foot more easily. After the wedding the bride gave each of the main female in-laws a pair at a special ceremony known as 'dividing the shoes'.

Like the binding methods, there were some regional differences. In general, those from the north, especially Beijing, had a 'bow' shape—an exaggerated curved sole and heel in one piece, often with leather reinforcements at toe and heel. In the late nineteenth and early twentieth centuries, style-conscious women from Shanghai, then the fashion capital of China, liked a multiple heel, while those from the southern provinces, such as Guangdong, wore shoes often made of black cotton or silk, with a fairly flat heel.

Some shoes had embroidered soles for wearing indoors while sitting on the *kang*. This was a low brick platform heated from below, found in most homes in northern China, where many activities took place. Shoes made for burial also had embroidered soles, but were usually made in blue or white, the colours of mourning. Miniature shoes, about 3 centimetres long, were worn when worshipping the Goddess of Seven Sisters in a festival held in the seventh lunar month, when unmarried girls made offerings to the goddess in the hope of finding a husband.

[PLATE 8]
Opposite: Bound feet shoes: top left, Shanghai style with multiple heel; top right, sleeping shoes with bells in the heels; bottom left, boots for use in the bedchamber; bottom right, pink satin flat shoes. Collection of the author.

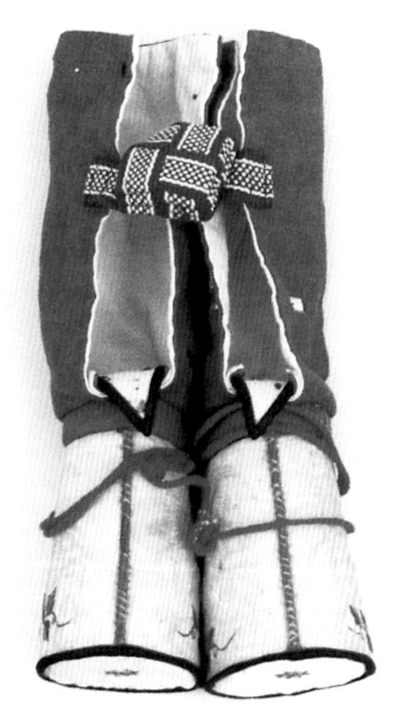
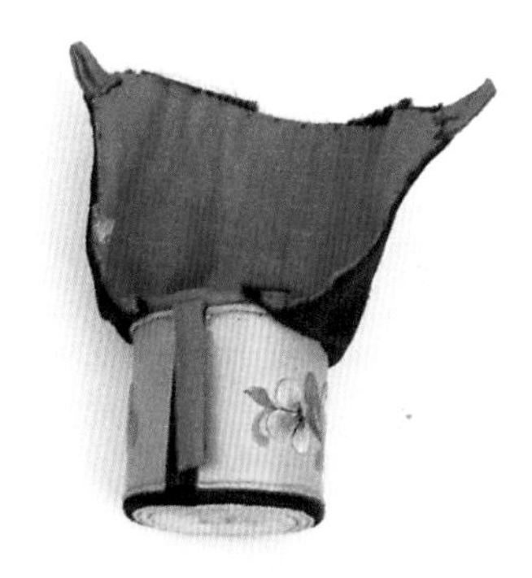

[PLATE 9]

Supports for bound feet: two pairs of separate supports with attached heel tongues; set of boots with inner heel supports and ankle covers. Collection of the author.

[PLATE 10]
Shoes in black cotton with open toes; a pair of cotton shoes with wooden heels. Collection of the author.

Plate 8 shows some different styles of bound feet shoes. One pair, embroidered on red satin with satin stitch and couched gold thread, has the multiple heel that became popular in Shanghai. Measuring 11 centimetres from heel to toe, they could have been worn by a bride on her wedding day. Sleeping shoes shown at the top right were also made of red satin, the colour thought to contrast best with the whiteness of the limbs. Made to be worn in the bedchamber, this pair has bells inside the heels to fuel erotic associations. The boots of red silk were also for use in the bedroom, and have lotus flowers and bats, symbols of purity, fruitfulness and happiness, embroidered in satin stitch and outlined with couched gold thread. The flat shoes in pink satin, embroidered with butterflies and the phoenix, measure 18 centimetres from heel to toe and were made at the beginning of the twentieth century for women who had had their feet bound for too long for them to regain natural size, and who could not wear normal shoes.

Raising the heel was said to make walking easier, but more importantly it made the foot seem even smaller. Supports for bound feet came in several guises. A woman could cheat by putting an inside support shaped like an embroidered cotton reel inside the boot. The heel of the foot was raised and secured with tapes around the lower leg. Boots with rigid ankle covers had metal stays inside to support the leg and conceal the bandages. **Plate 9** shows such a set of boots, with the ankle covers made of coarse blue cotton with metal stays and inner heel supports. Embroidered ankle covers were worn over the top. Other types of supports were visible and worn under the heel of the shoe, being tied through the three loops around the shoe, like the small pair with yellow embroidered heels, shown at top right. The other, larger pair of separate supports at top left is quite rare, being still unworn and having the woven blue and white cotton tapes untied. They came from the Shantou region and are as referred to above by Mrs. Little during her visit to that area. The pair of black cotton shoes at the botton of **Plate 10** has an integral wooden heel and is based on the same principle as mentioned. Once the heel was in place, only the toe of the shoe was visible under the trousers or skirt, giving the impression of small size and accentuating the rolling gait which men found so desirable.

The pair of shoes in **Plate 11** is documented as having been collected during the Pitt Amherst Embassy to China in 1816. The vamp is of red and yellow silk with an attached ankle cover of natural cotton, with loops for tapes to pass through to fasten around the leg. Separate green silk embroidered ankle covers are then worn over the shoes. There is a wooden shoe-last as part of the set, which would have been used to make other pairs the same size.

Iron or wooden studs were added in some cases to raise and protect the embroidered silk shoes from the dirt of the streets. Wooden clogs with leather straps over the foot were worn in bad weather by working women. **Plate 12** shows a shoe with an embroidered red and black cotton vamp and a wooden sole with metal cleats. The pair on the right has black leather vamps and soles and was made for a woman whose feet had

[PLATE 11]

Opposite: Set of shoes with ankle covers and a wooden last, collected during the Pitt Amherst Embassy to China in 1816. Collection of the author.

[PLATE 12]

Above: Shoe with iron cleats; pair of leather shoes for bound feet. Collection of the author.

[PLATE 13]

Opposite: Ankle covers in blue satin embroidered with a phoenix design. Collection of the author.

been bound; these were worn well into the twentieth century.

Ankle Covers, Socks and Puttees

As already mentioned, tube-like ankle covers or leggings were worn to cover bandages used for binding the feet. The ankle covers shown in **Plate 13** are in blue silk lined with cotton, and are embroidered with a phoenix amid flowers and butterflies. Leggings were made of silk with an embroidered hem which hung over the shoe. They were fastened with ties around the calf, and the under-trouser legs tucked inside the leggings. Bandages were changed after bathing, but the shoes and leggings or ankle covers were the last items of clothing to be removed inside the curtained bedchamber, the small feet and their smell being a strong aphrodisiac.

Plate 14 shows a pair of socks made of fine white cotton with cutaway heels, which were worn over the binding cloths. The tops of the socks were wide so they could be pulled over the foot, and were held in place with ribbons. The pair on the left is in peach silk padded and lined with cotton and embroidered with flowers and butterflies in the 'three blues', with cotton soles and heels. The third pair is made of pale green silk embroidered with black, with deep blue soles and a cutaway heel.

Puttees were tied around the ankle covers and the bottom of the trousers. Shorter than men's, they measured about 5 centimetres wide and between 70 and 80 centimetres long. Those shown in **Plate 15** are made of tightly woven pale green silk with fringing at each end, and embroidered at one end with a design of flowers and figures in a garden. The other pair are in red silk with blue embroidered flowers and butterflies, with bells and fringing at the ends.

Shoes for Natural Feet

Not all women bound their feet. In southern China, especially in Guangdong and Hong Kong, women from the Hakka ethnic group had natural feet and, like those women who had been persuaded to give up footbinding, wore normal-sized shoes. "At Canton [Guangzhou] the women with natural feet wear what is called the boat shoe, being shaped like the bottom of a boat, on which they can balance backwards and forwards. Boatwomen and working women do

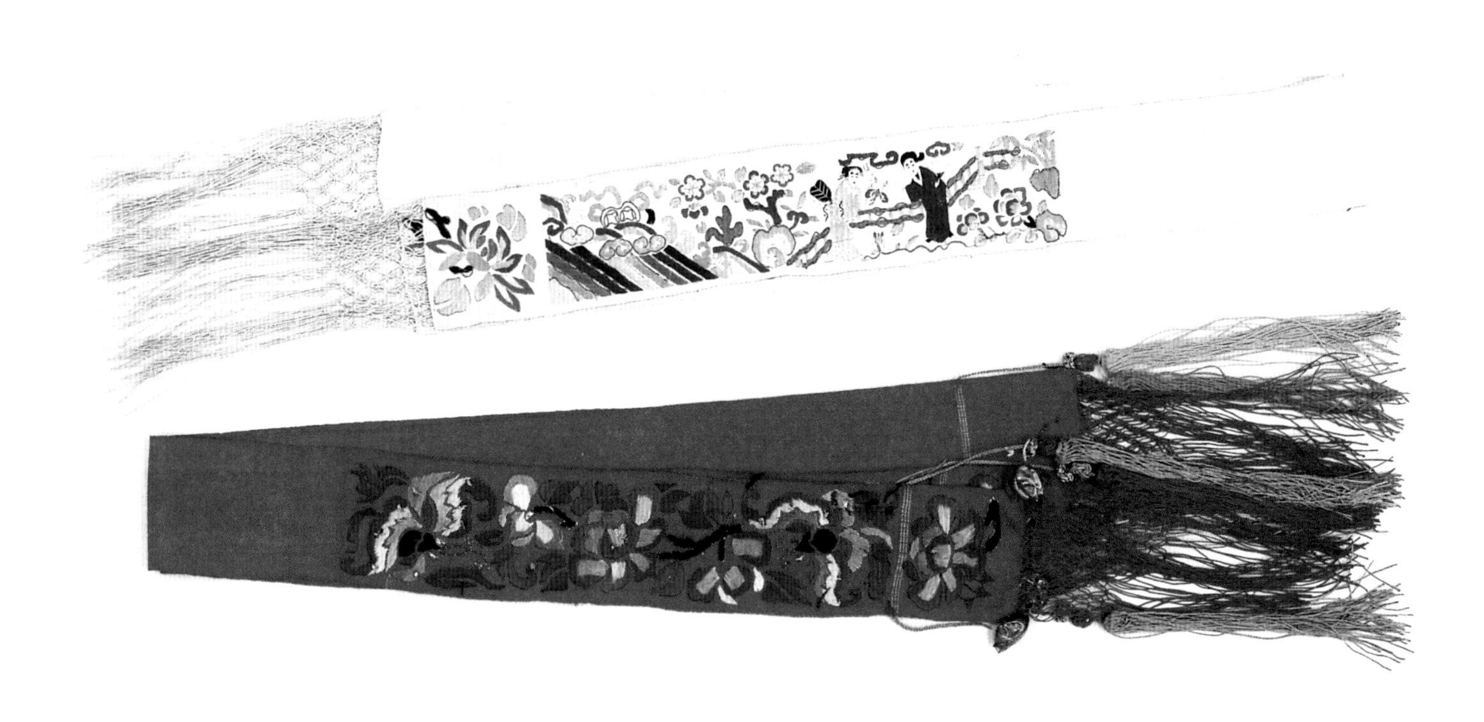

[PLATE 14]

Opposite: Three pairs of socks: peach silk padded and lined, with cotton soles; blue silk with cutaway heels; fine cotton with cutaway heels. Collection of the author.

[PLATE 15]

Above: Two pairs of silk puttees. Collection of the author.

not bind there, which has given the foreigner, who so often gets his idea of a Chinese city from Canton, the impression that this is the case all through China. Alas! in the West [of China] women even track boats with bound, hoof-like feet, besides carrying water, whilst in the north the unfortunate working women do field work, often kneeling on the heavy clay soil, because they are incapable of standing. . . . The more distinguished ladies in Hong Kong or Canton who do not bind, wear the Manchu clog-like shoe —with a very high heel in the centre of the foot."[9]

Figure 6 shows a woman in southern China with tiny bound feet, while her servant has natural feet. The servant is wearing shoes with thick soles similar to those in **Plate 16**, which shows a pair of flat shoes with a vamp of purple silk embroidered in Peking knot with flowers and a phoenix, and a sole made of layers of paper plus one of leather.

CHILDREN'S FOOTWEAR

Shoes for Young Children

Very young children wore silk bootees which sometimes had ties that fastened around the ankle to hold them in place, as can be seen in Chapter 3, **Figure 7**. When the child was transported in a baby carrier worn on the bearer's back, these bootees looked quite colourful as the child approached. As seen here at the top left of **Plate 17**, they were made of red, purple or orange satin embroidered with a four-clawed dragon, which was a protector from evil. Other designs were of a phoenix, fish or deer. Often padded animals and birds were suspended above the toe on

[FIG 6]

Above: Chinese woman with bound feet and her servant with natural feet.

[PLATE 16]

Opposite: Shoes for natural feet with thick soles and embroidered vamps. Collection of the author.

[PLATE 17]

Opposite: Two pairs of children's bootees; animal shoes in the design of a pig and a tiger. Collection of the author.

[PLATE 18]

Below: Bound feet shoes for a young girl; a model of a girl's bound foot and its matching shoe from Fujian Province. Collection of the author.

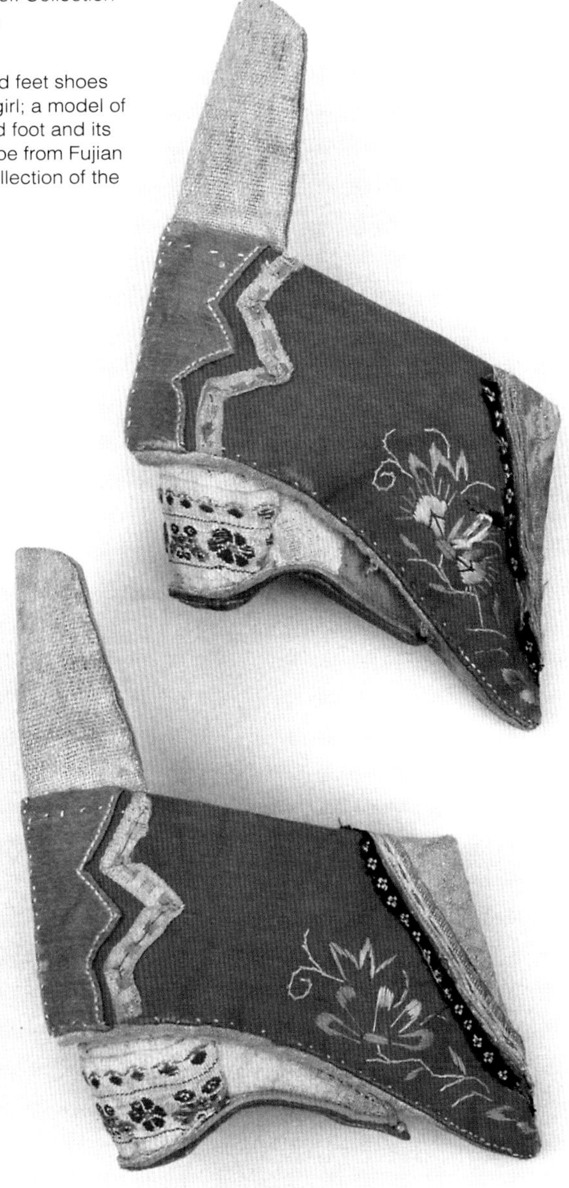

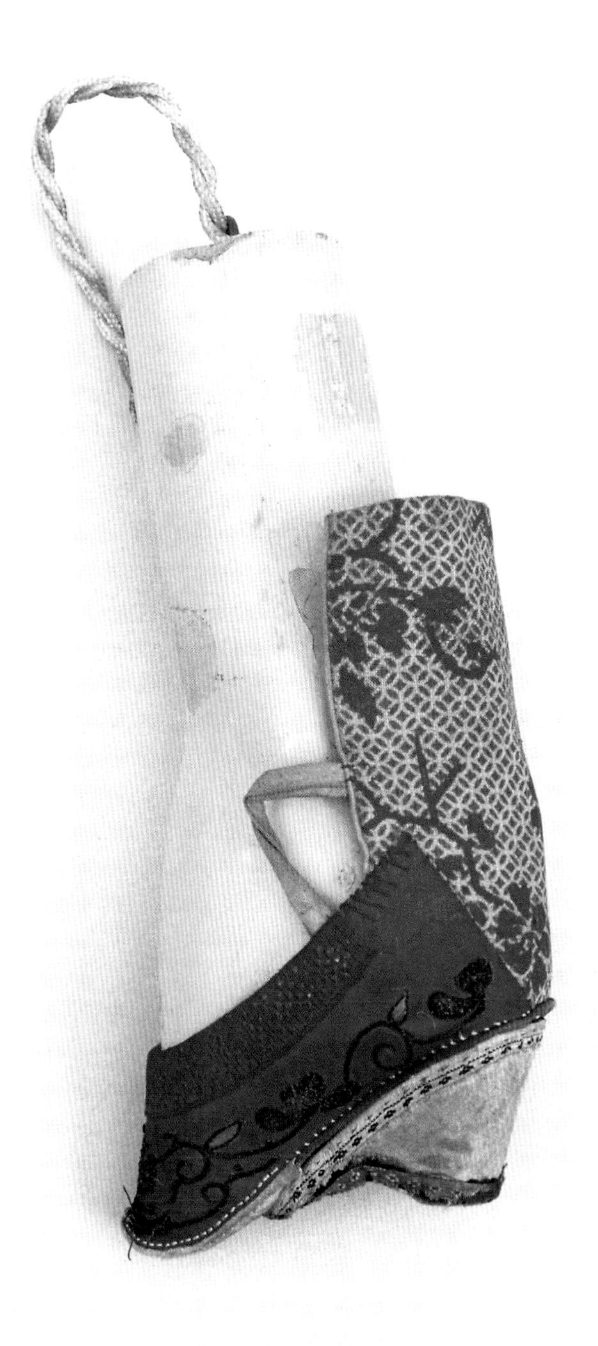

[PLATE 19]

Opposite: Boy's black satin shoes; woven straw shoes. Collection of the author.

wires—in this case, a three-legged toad. Long coloured tassels hung from the front, together with multi-coloured pom-poms.

Like other accessories, children's footwear was also made in the form of a dog, cat, tiger, or pig for protection and good fortune. Large eyes to see evil lurking, large furry ears to hear it, and whiskers all helped to suggest the creature being represented. Usually made of red cotton or satin, with a brightly embroidered vamp and padded cotton sole, some shoes even had bells on the toes to produce an audible warning for the spirits. In **Figure 2**, one of the sons of the prince is wearing shoes made to resemble an animal. **Plate 17** shows a pair of shoes made to represent a pig, while the pair at bottom left is in the design of a tiger. The red satin bootees have a design of lotus flowers, bats and the *shou* character on the toes.

Shoes for Older Children

When a girl was of the proper age, she would begin to have her feet bound and to wear tiny embroidered shoes. **Plate 18** shows a shoe on a plaster of Paris mould of a bound foot, the attached label identifying it as being a "Baptist Missionary Society demonstration model" from Fujian Province. It would have been used in the nineteenth century to demonstrate footbinding, possibly as part of the fight by missionary societies to abolish the custom. The shoe is made of red silk with a cotton heel tongue and loops. The pair on the left measures 9 centimetres from heel to toe and is made of brown silk with a cotton heel tongue; they would have been worn by a very young girl.

Shoes for older boys were made of satin with a thick white sole, similar to those worn by men. Like those illustrated on the left in **Plate 19**, the vamp was sometimes embroidered with auspicious flowers and insects, and had a centre seam reinforced with leather that extended over the rigid sole to give sufficient spring for walking. Another style, seen on the right of **Plate 19**, was made in woven straw, for use in summer in the southern provinces.

Endnotes

1 H. C. Sirr, *China and the Chinese,* W. S. Orr & Co., pub. 1849, rpt Chinese Materials Center, Inc. 1979, vol.1, p. 309.

2 Verity Wilson, *Chinese Dress,* pub. Victoria & Albert Museum, London, 1986, p. 29.

3 *Kowtow* literally means 'to knock the head'. A full *kowtow* required the person to kneel three times, one after another, each time knocking the head three times on the ground.

4 Alexander Hosie, *Manchuria, Its People, Resources and Recent History,* London, Metheun & Co., 1904, p. 157.

5 Mrs. Archibald Little, *The Land of the Blue Gown,* T. Fisher Unwin, London, 1902, p. 339–40.

6 *Ibid.*, p. 340.

7 S. Wells Williams, *The Middle Kingdom,* pub. 1895, rpt Paragon Book Reprint Corp., New York, 1966, vol. 1, p. 768.

8 Bound feet shoes are popular with collectors today, and their scarcity means they are now being copied. These copies are usually made from a larger piece of embroidered silk cut to shape for the vamp. The soles are made from a few layers of coarse cotton or even moulded from plaster of Paris.

9 Mrs. Archibald Little, *The Land of the Blue Gown,* p. 343.

~ *Chapter Eight* ~

Home Furnishings and Accessories

THE IMPERIAL COURT

The Forbidden City in Beijing, the imperial court of the Qing emperors with their consorts, concubines, eunuchs and attendants, was built in the Ming dynasty between 1406 and 1420. Measuring some 900 metres from north to south, and over 700 metres from east to west, the high walls, surrounded by a moat, had only four gates. Three of the gates led into the southern section, where the major official buildings were sited. The fourth, the Outer Gate, was situated in the north, where the residential section consisted of many palaces separated by courtyards.

In the centre of the Forbidden City were three great ceremonial halls, set one behind the other. The largest and most notable of these was the Hall of the Supreme Harmony *(Taihedian)*. This was the setting for important state events, such as the festivities at the Lunar New Year, the emperor's birthday, and most momentous of all, the emperor's enthronement, an occasion so sacred that his ascent to the throne was veiled from the gaze of such mere mortals as the nobles and officials waiting outside.

Cushion Covers

The Throne Room was a cavernous room with a black marble tiled floor and tall golden columns reaching up to a coffered ceiling intricately decorated in black, gold, blue and cinnabar red. Deep within the hall, in solitary splendour, out of sight of all but the very highest members of the court, stood the Dragon Throne. The wide, elaborately carved golden throne was placed on a high platform reached by seven steps, in front of a seven-panelled, gilded screen carved with more dragons. The seat of the throne was covered with a large, flat, rectangular cushion like that shown in **Plate 1**. This imperial yellow cushion cover, dating from the Qianlong reign, has four pairs of profile five-clawed dragons chasing a flaming pearl, and one central front-facing dragon, all embroidered in couched gold thread. Dispersed across the background are clouds embroidered in satin stitch, while the border has a *li shui* design.

Slightly less ornate dragon thrones were placed within the other ceremonial halls and palaces, standing in front of a five- or three-panelled screen. On some thrones, where the carving was less ornate, a shaped cushion was added at the back of the chair. Seen in **Plate 2** is a splendid cushion made during the reign of the Daoguang Emperor. The main panel contains the Eight Buddhist emblems against a background of the *wan* motif, while the border is embroidered with flowers and bats repeated again in the centre medallion. At each side was an elbow rest, as seen

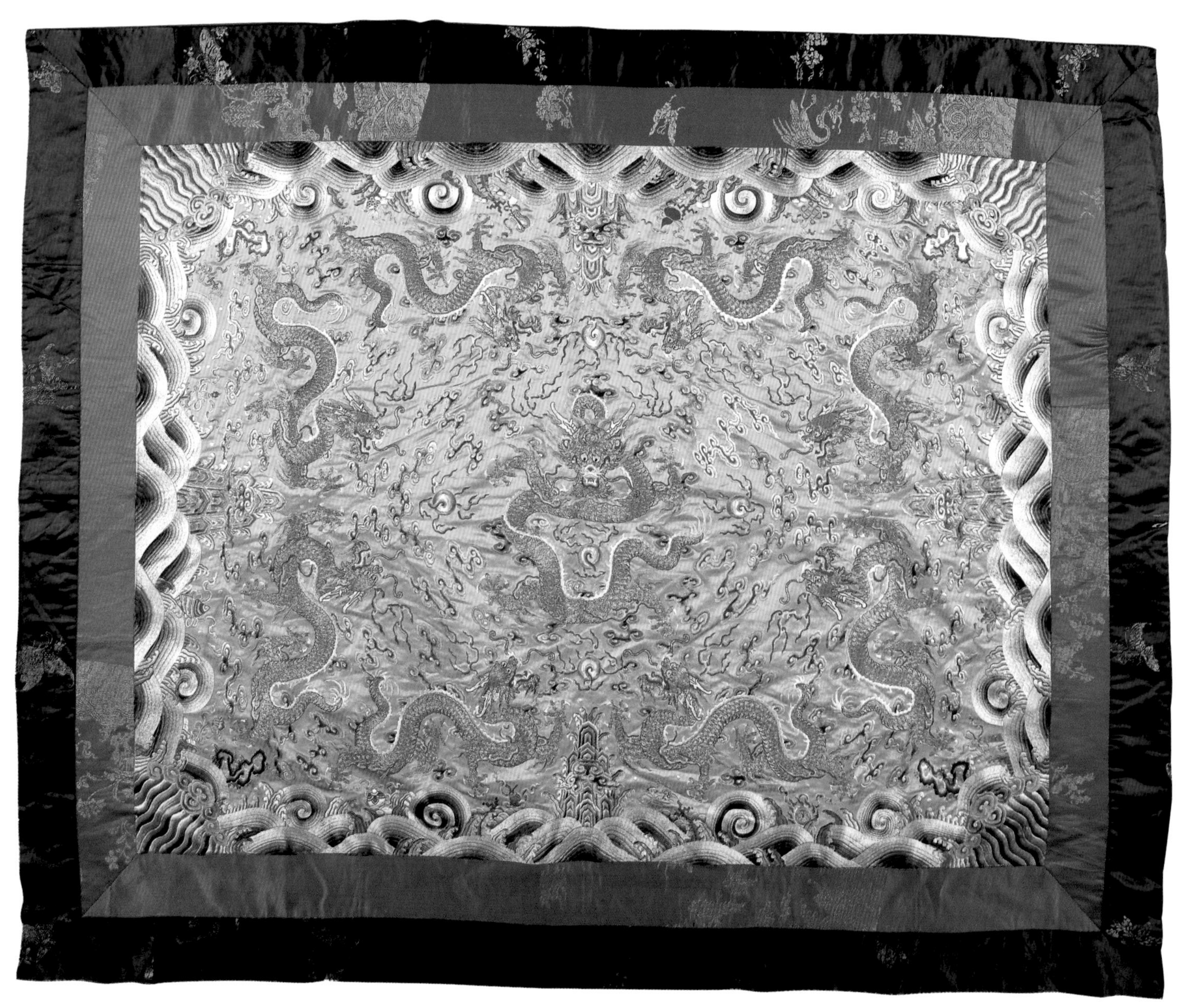

[PLATE 1]

An imperial yellow cushion cover with four pairs of profile five-clawed dragons and one central front-facing dragon, all embroidered in couched gold thread, 114 cm x 85.5 cm; Qianlong reign. Plum Blossoms (Int'l) Ltd, Hong Kong.

[PLATE 2]

Shaped throne cushion. The central panel contains the Eight Buddhist emblems against a background of the *wan* motif, while the border is embroidered with flowers and bats to match the centre medallion, 85 cm x 73 cm, Daoguang reign. Linda Wrigglesworth, London.

[PLATE 3]

Right: Three elbow rest cushions: the centre one has bats, peaches, lotus flowers and a sacred fungus embroidered on yellow silk, 20 cm square, Daoguang reign; the pair of silk brocade cushions have lotus flowers in red, orange and purple, 25 cm square, Guangxu reign. Linda Wrigglesworth, London.

[PLATE 4]

Opposite: A throne cushion embroidered with long life emblems on a yellow silk ground. The central roundel of nine peaches is surrounded by twenty-four cranes and clouds with a border of mountains and sea waves, 129.5 cm square, eighteenth century. Spink & Son, Ltd, London.

in **Plate 3**. The centre one, dating from the Daoguang period, has bats, peaches, lotus flowers and the sacred fungus embroidered on yellow silk, while the pair of silk brocade cushions have lotus flowers in red, orange and purple and date from the Guangxu reign. On the seat would be a square cushion like the one in **Plate 4**. This superbly embroidered throne cushion is worked with numerous long life emblems on a yellow silk ground. The central roundel of nine peaches is surrounded by twenty-four cranes and clouds with a border of mountains and sea waves.

Many of the day-to-day affairs of state were dealt with in the halls and palaces to the rear of the ceremonial halls. The emperor's office, where he attended to routine matters and gave daily audience to officials, was within the Hall of Mental Cultivation *(Yangxindian)*, seen here in **Plate 5**. For a palace, the room is quite simply furnished. On the *kang* placed against the wall, the imperial yellow shaped cushion to support the back and the large yellow rectangular cushion on the seat indicate the regal occupier. Low tables hold memorials and other matters of business; panels on the walls contain calligraphy; and books add a sense of purpose to the room.

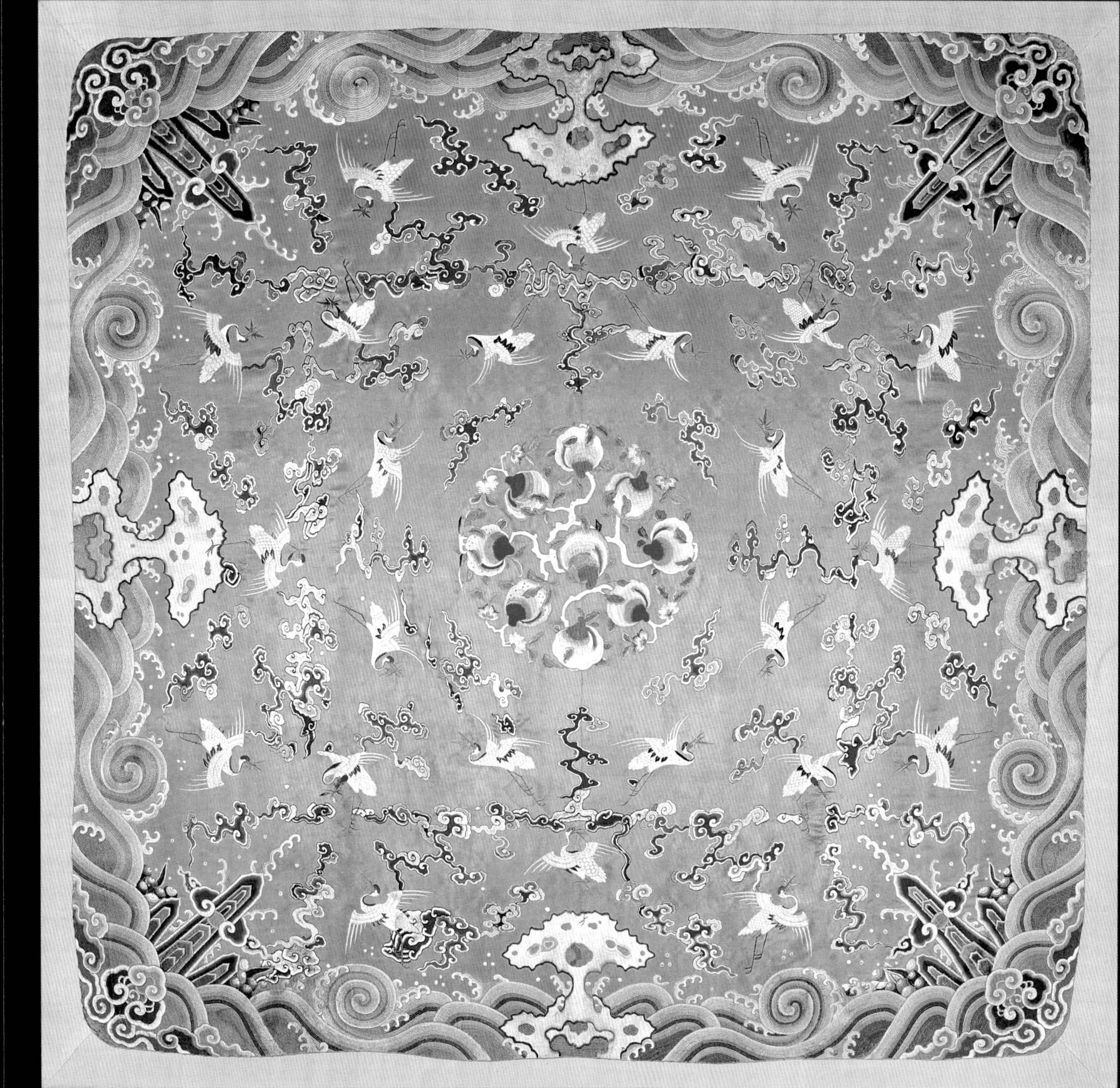

[PLATE 5]

Above: The emperor's office in the Hall of Mental Cultivation in the Forbidden City in Beijing, simply furnished with the *kang* on which are placed a yellow shaped cushion to support the back, a large yellow rectangular cushion (on the seat) and two elbow rest cushions.

[PLATE 6]

Opposite: Yellow brocade wall hanging with five four-clawed dragons, 135 cm x 120 cm; early eighteenth century. Altfield Gallery, Hong Kong.

Wall Hangings and Table Covers

To add warmth, especially in the bitterly cold winters in the north, wall hangings and door curtains were hung around the rooms to keep out draughts. These hangings of embroidered silk or tapestry were also covered with lucky symbols. Birds and flowers, landscape and genre scenes, figures from history and folklore, and above all, objects and characters with auspicious connotations formed the basis of the motifs used.

Plate 6 shows a yellow brocade panel, possibly made for an imperial prince; it dates to the early eighteenth century. Four profile and one facing four-clawed dragons grasp flaming pearls in a cloud-filled sky. Dispersed in the background are many lanterns, suggesting that the hanging was made for the Lantern Festival held two weeks after the Lunar New Year.

The pale yellow *kang* table cover shown in **Plate 7** was probably used in the female quarters of the imperial household, as the phoenix in the centre is the symbol of the empress. The background is of clouds, bats and the *wan* symbol, while the border has peonies and foliage. It dates from the reign of the Tongzhi Emperor (1862–1874).

The Bedchamber

Within the same compound as the *Yangxindian* were the emperor's private quarters, which included his bedchamber. Attended by female servants and some three thousand eunuchs (preferred because of their inability to sire children, thus ensuring the purity of the progeniture), the emperor was the only man to

萬
壽

[PLATE 7]

Kang table cover for the female imperial household embroidered with the phoenix against a background of clouds, bats and the *wan* symbol, while the border has peonies and foliage, 137 cm x 104 cm; Tongzhi reign. Linda Wrigglesworth, London. Detail shown left.

[PLATE 8]
Bedchamber of the emperor within the *Yangxindian*.

spend the night in the Forbidden City. His wives, consorts and many concubines allowed him to produce sufficient offspring to ensure the succession: the Kangxi Emperor, for example, sired thirty-five sons among his fifty-six children.

A lady-in-waiting, Princess Der Ling, describes making up the bed of the Empress Dowager Cixi. The bed itself was made of elaborately carved wood with a piece of felt placed over the bedboard. "Then three thick mattresses made of yellow brocade were placed over the felt. After this came the sheets made of different colored soft silk, and over the whole thing was placed a covering of plain yellow satin embroidered with gold dragons and blue clouds. She had a great many pillows, all beautifully embroidered, which were placed on the bed during the daytime; but had a particular one stuffed with tea leaves on which she slept. It is said that stuffing the pillow . . . with tea leaves is good for the eyes. . . .

"Besides this last yellow embroidered cover, there were six covers of different colors, pale mauve, blue, pink, green and violet, [that] were placed one on top of the other. Over the top of the bed was a frame of wood handsomely carved and from this frame white crepe curtains, beautifully embroidered, hung, and numerous little gauze silk bags filled with scent [musk] were suspended. . . ."[1]

In **Plate 8** the emperor's bed is shown festooned with curtains, which were tied back during the day. Folded neatly at the back of the bed are coverlets in various colours and designs. Sword-shaped streamers hang at each side of the bed, the shape designed to protect the occupants from harm. The rest of the room is furnished with embroidered wall hangings, lanterns hung with tassels, a side table and ornaments.

THE HOME OF AN OFFICIAL OR WEALTHY MERCHANT

The residences of princes and officials were enclosed within a walled complex called a *yamen* that contained both offices and living quarters, built around a quadrangle with a central courtyard. The Regulations even extended to the number of rooms and the type of gates the prince, nobleman or official could have. For instance, "In the 9th year of the reign of Shunzhi, it was stipulated that [the] 'Main entrance of residence of prince is 5-bay across with 3 pairs of doors . . . 63 golden knobs on each panelling, . . . topped by green-glazed tiles.'"[2] The gates of the sons of princes and those of a lower degree had correspondingly fewer knobs and pairs of doors.

The rooms in a traditional Chinese residence would be viewed by westerners today as uncomfortable and little suited to relaxation away from the affairs of state and commerce. Furniture was upright, hard, unyielding and, together with the high ceilings, added to the solemn and formal look of the rooms. The living room belonging to a wealthy merchant in Guangzhou in the late nineteenth century is seen in **Figure 1.** Wooden chairs line the walls, interspersed with small, square, high tables on which to put a water pipe or ornament, while spittoons are placed underneath. In the centre of the room is a table where the family would sit to eat. The stools around the table have cool marble panels set into

[FIG 1]
The living room belonging to a wealthy merchant in Guangzhou, late nineteenth century.

[PLATE 9]

Left: Chair cover of black silk embroidered with four four-clawed dragons in couched gold thread and peacock feathor clouds, eighteenth century. Teresa Coleman Fine Arts, Hong Kong.

[PLATE 10]

Opposite: A pair of navy blue silk chair covers, one embroidered with a scholar seated at a table within a pavilion, while in the other ladies approach a pavilion bearing offerings, 55.5 cm x 195 cm, eighteenth century. Spink & Son Ltd, London.

the seat for greater comfort in the hot summers of southern China. Hanging lanterns lit by oil illuminate the room, and small bonsai trees, jade ornaments, a clock, and calligraphy panels complete the furnishings.

Chair Covers

For ceremonial occasions, or when important visitors were received, chairs would be covered by long rectangular covers, made in pairs, plain or embroidered as appropriate. Like the court robes, the colours and designs on these covers and cushions indicated rank. **Plate 9** shows a striking example of four four-clawed dragons embroidered in couched gold thread with peacock feather clouds on a black silk ground. The topmost dragon hung down at the back of the chair; the occupant of the chair sat with his back to the largest dragon; and the two profile ones were behind each foot. Dating from the eighteenth century, it would have been used in the home of a wealthy nobleman or mandarin. **Plate 10** shows a pair of navy blue silk chair covers for a less formal occasion. One is embroidered with a scholar seated at a table within a pavilion, while in the other ladies approach a pavilion bearing offerings. At the top of each is a phoenix in flight, on the seat is an archaic dragon roundel, and at the foot, a *qilin*.

Birthday Hangings

Age is revered in the east, and for Chinese people the sixtieth birthday was the first in their adult life to be celebrated in a grand manner. At this

[PLATE 11]

Right: A heavenly maiden with a deer holding the sacred fungus from the central part of a large birthday hanging in red silk embroidered with floss silk satin stitch, 1927. Collection of the author.

[PLATE 12]

Opposite: Pair of hanging decorations for the bed, showing dragon boats, each with five women holding lotus flowers and melons, all symbols of fruitfulness; umbrellas and flags carry the names of candidates with the highest marks in the imperial examinations. Collection of the author.

stage a person was considered to have lived through a complete set of five twelve-year cycles. The seventieth, eightieth and ninetieth birthdays were also scenes of much homage and respect. On these occasions it was the custom to have a large panel embroidered with many longevity emblems to commemorate the event.

One such panel, approximately 180 centimetres wide by 300 centimetres long, was made to hang in the main hall, where the celebrations took place. In the central panel, seen in **Plate 11**, which alone measures 104 centimetres wide and 170 centimetres in length, a heavenly maiden is holding a peach, a bat flies down towards her, while at her feet is a deer holding a sprig of sacred fungus in its mouth. Most of the embroidery is done in satin stitch using silk floss thread with couched thread to outline areas. The ground cloth is of red silk, a most auspicious colour for this occasion. Chinese characters, embroidered in couched gold thread on the right side of the figure, announce it was made for Madam Cheung, a lady who was a model of good conduct, and on whose eightieth birthday would be held a great celebration in the Autumn, season of the Chrysanthemum, in the sixteenth year of the Republic (1927). Characters written in black ink list the name of her husband's company and business associates, followed by her twenty-two grandchildren. The Eight Immortals, two of which are shown in Chapter 2, **Plates 14 and 15**, are arranged in two groups at each side, and the Queen Mother of the Western Heavens is depicted in the scene above the central maiden.

Bedchamber Furnishings

Bedchambers were furnished simply, with the bed taking up most of the room. The Chinese wedding bed was a structure made to give maximum privacy to the couple, often with a small antechamber down the longer side in front of the sleeping section to enable them to retreat from a populous household. Hangings for the back of the bed had scenes designed to promote fertility and the birth of many sons. A narrow curtain ran along the top, and curtains all around gave seclusion, as well as keeping out draughts: those on the side were held back with decorative

百

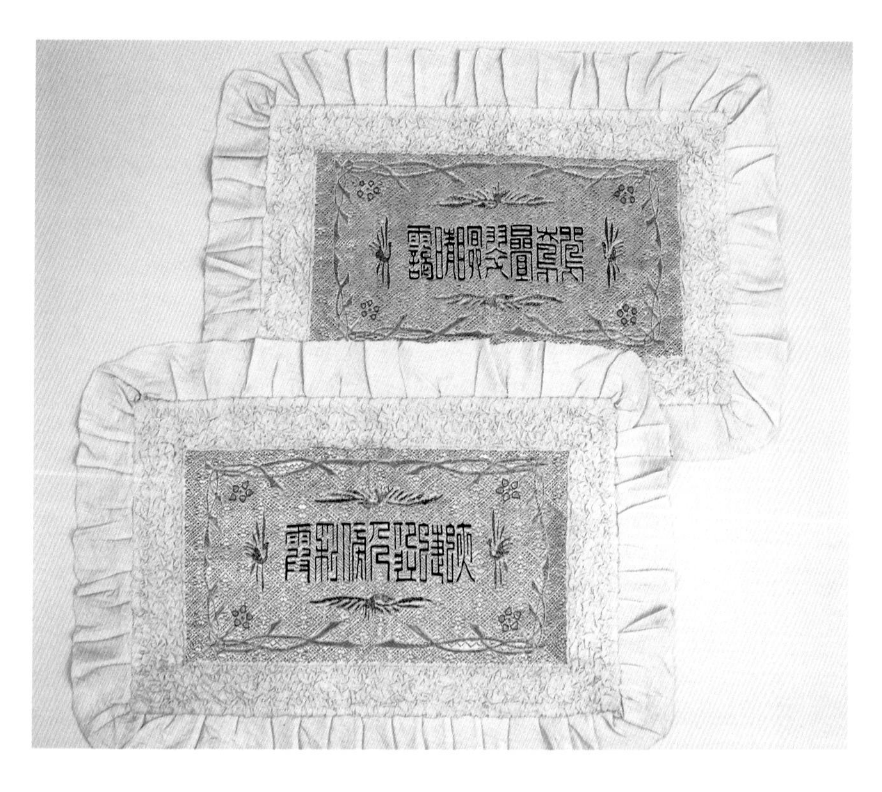

[PLATE 13]

Above: Pair of pillowcases with voided brick stitch design of flowers and phoenixes surrounding auspicious Chinese characters connected with marriage, Shanghai, early twentieth century. Collection of the author.

[PLATE 14]

Opposite: A set of four pillow ends from hard rectangular pillows, which tell the story of a candidate entering and successfully returning from the imperial examinations. Collection of the author.

metal or embroidered hooks. A curtain across the door of the room kept out more draughts. Other furniture would include a dressing table and stool, a clothes rack and a washstand.

Hanging Decorations

At each side of the bed hung sword-shaped decorations like those seen in **Plate 7**, or three-dimensional decorations, often intended as fertility symbols. The pair shown in **Plate 12** are dragon boats, each with five women seated inside holding lotus flowers and melons, symbols of fruitfulness. The umbrellas and flags on the boat suggest those used by important officials, and carry the names of the candidates with the best results in the imperial examinations.

Pillowcases

Naturally the bed coverlet and pillowcases had many auspicious symbols, such as mandarin ducks—the emblem of marital fidelity—embroidered on them. **Plate 13** shows a pair of pillowcases from Shanghai, dating from the early twentieth century. The frill and edging is of turquoise ruched silk, with centres of pink voided brick stitch with flowers and phoenixes surrounding auspicious Chinese characters connected with marriage. Other types of pillows were hard rectangular shapes placed underneath the neck, often made of glazed ceramic or woven bamboo. Cloth-covered ones had small embroidered squares at each end of the pillow. Those shown in **Plate 14** are intended for the two pillows for husband and wife. They tell the story of a candidate entering, and successfully returning from, the imperial examinations, a wish for sons who do well in life.

Small Accessories

Most of the small items used around the home were embroidered. Mirrors, made first of highly polished bronze and later glass, took several shapes, the most common being oval or round. They were kept in embroidered covers on the dressing table. **Plate 15** shows an oval cover with embroidery in voided satin stitch of a child wearing a *doudou* and sitting under a lotus flower, a very popular fertility symbol. **Plate 16** shows a padded cover for a circular bronze mirror with the design of a boy riding a deer, again a wish for wealth and distinction.

Small, round, embroidered cloth pads were used to wipe hair oil on a woman's head to keep

[PLATE 15]

Right: Oval mirror cover embroidered in voided satin stitch of a child wearing a *doudou* and sitting under a lotus flower, a very popular fertility symbol. Collection of the author.

[PLATE 16]

Opposite: Round mirror cover in voided satin stitch with the design of a boy riding a deer, a wish for wealth and distinction. Collection of the author.

the hair in place, or to apply makeup. The set in **Plate 17** is of embroidered felt, while the other pair has a geometric flower design. **Plate 18** shows a wrist cushion or pulse rest, made to be placed under a woman's wrist when consulting a doctor. The top and underside are in serviceable blue cotton, while the sides (in silk) have auspicious 'four character' phrases, such as 'clouds bring good fortune', 'peace and safety every month' and, on the light blue background, 'red plum blossoms blooming in the snow', heralding spring and the start of another year.

Other items on display in the main living rooms were photograph frames, which became popular once the camera became universally available. The apertures are very small, reflecting the size of photographs of the time. The one in **Plate 19** is embroidered with green voided satin stitch with the characters for 'picture' above the photograph. The other photograph frame is in cream silk with the design of a vine. Also in **Plate 19** is a silk embroidered chopstick container from Shanghai, which hung on the wall. **Plate 20** shows a candle holder with twelve red felt petals, each embroidered with flowers and butterflies. The inner green and lilac petals are in the design of a lotus flower. Finally, cases were made to hold a pair of scissors and followed the shape of Chinese scissors, which had large round handles. They were made in various sizes to match the scissor sizes, and sometimes had a pocket halfway down into which the scissors were tucked. The one shown in **Plate 21** is in red silk with the design of a lotus flower and a butterfly, while on the reverse is a peony and a phoenix.

[PLATE 17]

Opposite: Two pairs of embroidered cloth pads used to apply hair oil or makeup. Collection of the author.

[PLATE 18]

Above: Wrist cushion or pulse rest with blue cotton top and bottom, and silk sides embroidered with 'four character' auspicious sayings. Judith Rutherford.

Endnotes

[1] Princess Der Ling, *Two Years in the Forbidden City*, Moffat, Yard & Co, New York, 1914, p. 62–3.

[2] *Quadrangles of Beijing*, Beijing Arts and Photography Publishing House, 1993, p. 11.

[PLATE 19]

Above: Two embroidered photograph frames and a silk embroidered chopstick container, Shanghai, circa 1920. Collection of the author.

[PLATE 20]

Opposite, left: Candle holder in the shape of a lotus flower. Collection of the author.

[PLATE 21]

Opposite, right: Scissors case in red silk with the design of a lotus flower and butterfly embroidered in satin stitch. Judith Rutherford.

Care and Maintenance

Most accessory items are quite easy to care for as long as some common sense is applied. Always buy the best available in terms of condition: a soiled item may be cheaper, but it will never give the same long term enjoyment. There are times when a piece is so rare or very old that condition becomes of secondary importance. In that case, advice from a professional textile conservator should be taken regarding repairs, cleaning, storage and display. But some form of care and maintenance should be undertaken to preserve any collection. If it is simply a favourite piece that does not have too much intrinsic value there are some easy steps which can be taken to clean and help preserve it.

Always wash the hands before handling any textile pieces; in fact, it is advisable to get in the habit of handling good pieces with white cotton gloves. First brush the accessory with a soft brush to loosen surface dust; a hand held vacuum cleaner will bring out more dirt. If there are loose threads, place a nylon stocking over the mouth of the cleaner to prevent the threads from being sucked up and unravelling even more. Steaming the piece gently with distilled water in a travel steamer sometimes releases more dust and dirt. Before trying this, however, test for colour fastness of the embroidery dyes. To do this, place a drop of distilled water on a coloured area and press using a piece of white cotton cloth; if no colour appears, it is probably safe to continue. Finally, catch down loose threads using a fine needle and matching silk thread and press lightly.

Small pieces can be stored flat in a drawer or cupboard, wrapped in acid free tissue paper. Stuff shoes or hats with tissue paper to help them hold their shape. Ideally the temperature should be between 65° and 75°F (18°–24°C) and the humidity level between 50 and 60 percent. If high humidity is a problem, a dehumidifier will help; too low humidity is rarely a factor. The important consideration is to avoid rapid changes of temperature and humidity, which cause swelling and shrinking of the fibres. In fact, some of the oldest textiles have been wonderfully preserved in a natural environment. Many Ming robes and insignia badges, and even earlier pieces from the Song and Yuan dynasties were brought out of Tibet in the 1980s, some with the colours still fresh and vibrant. They had been kept, since they were presented to the Tibetans some four to five hundred years ago, in the dark, dry and cold conditions of the monasteries.

If the piece is to be framed it should be mounted on acid-free mat board. Check with the framer whether he can provide this. If the mat board is not acid-free, the cut edges of the board will discolour after a few years. When framing, choose a day when the air is quite dry and not humid, as moisture can be trapped behind the glass and will cause the piece to grow mould. If mildew does occur, remove the piece from the frame and kill the mould growth by placing the item on a clean flat surface outdoors on a sunny day with less than 50 percent humidity. Mould can also be killed by using a low power setting on a portable hairdryer held some 30 centimetres away from the piece. Some textile conservators decry the use of glass over embroidery, saying that it should be left exposed. They advocate gently brushing the loose dust from the piece from time to time. Others feel that the piece is safer behind glass, as long as the glass does not touch the object: at least a 1-centimetre gap should be left.

After framing, don't hang the piece facing direct sunlight, as even weak northern sun will fade textiles quite rapidly. Hang it, if possible, on an inside wall, that is to say one that is not exposed to the elements outside. If care is not taken, mould may build up between the back of the frame and the outside wall, which can penetrate through to the embroidery. Ideally textiles should only be exposed to artificial light or the ultraviolet rays from sunlight for short periods of time, say three to four months of the year. This can be seen as an opportunity to rotate one's collection, giving added enjoyment and at the same time preserving these mementoes of history for generations to come.

Further Reading

Catalogue of the Exhibition of Ch'ing Dynasty Costume Accessories, National Palace Museum, Taipei, 1986.

DICKINSON, G. & WRIGGLESWORTH, L, *Imperial Wardrobe*, Hong Kong, Oxford University Press, 1990.

EBERHARD, Wolfram, *A Dictionary of Chinese Symbols*, Routledge & Kegan Paul, London and New York, 1986.

GARRETT, Valery M., *Mandarin Squares: Mandarins and their Insignia*, Oxford University Press, Hong Kong, 1990.

GARRETT, Valery M., *Chinese Clothing: an Illustrated Guide*, Oxford University Press, Hong Kong, 1994.

Jewellery and Accessories of The Royal Consorts of Ch'ing Dynasty, Forbidden City Publishing House, Peking, and Parco Publishing Company, Hong Kong, 1992.

LEVY, Howard S., *Chinese Footbinding: The History of a Curious Erotic Custom,* Bell Publishing Company, New York, 1967.

MAILAND, Harold F., *Considerations for the Care of Textiles and Costumes: a Handbook for the Non-Specialist*, pub. Indianapolis Museum of Art, 1980.

VOLLMER, John E., *Decoding Dragons*, University of Oregon Museum of Art, Eugene, 1983.

WANG, Loretta H., *The Chinese Purse*, Hilit Publishing Co Ltd, Taiwan, 1986.

WANG Yarong, *Chinese Folk Embroidery*, Thames and Hudson Ltd., London, 1987.

WILLIAMS, C.A.S., *Outlines of Chinese Symbolism and Art Motives*, Customs College Press, Peking, 1931.

WILSON, Verity, *Chinese Dress*, Victoria and Albert Museum, London, 1986.

Sources of Illustrations

Care has been taken to trace and acknowledge the source of illustrations, but in some instances this has not been possible. Where indicated photographs were provided by, or reproduced with the kind permission of the Cleveland Museum of Art, Ohio; Library of Congress, Washington; National Palace Museum, Taipei, Taiwan, Republic of China; Palace Museum, Beijing; Urban Council Hong Kong from the collection of the Hong Kong Museum of Art; University of Oregon, Museum of Art. The photographs not listed are in the collection of the author.

Bland, J.O.P.and Backhouse E., *China Under the Empress Dowager*, Henri Vetch, Peking, 1939: Chapter 7, Fig 5

Burkhardt,V.R., *Chinese Creeds and Customs*, vols.1-3 South China Morning Post, Hong Kong, (1955-9): Chapter 2, Fig 2,3,4

Cleveland Museum of Art, Ohio: Chapter 3, Plate 6. Lang Shih-ning [Guiseppe Castiglione], Chinese, 1688–1768, Qing Dynasty. *Inauguration Portraits of Emperor Qianlong, The Empress, and the Eleven Imperial Consorts* (detail), 1736. Handscroll, ink and color on silk, 52.9 x 688.3 cm. © The Cleveland Museum of Art, 1996, John L. Severance Fund, 1969.31.

Der Ling, Princess, *Two Years in the Forbidden City,* Moffat, Yard & Co., New York, 1914: Chapter 6, Fig 1

Hardy, Rev. E.J., *John Chinaman at Home,* Unwin, London, 1905: Chapter 3, Fig 5; Chapter 6, Fig 2

Headland, I.T., *Chinese Mother Goose Rhymes,* Fleming H.Revell Co, New York, 1900: Chapter 3, Fig 7

Headland, I.T., *Court Life in China,* Fleming H.Revell Co, New York, 1909: Chapter 3, Fig 6

Hosie, Lady, *Two Gentlemen of China,* Seeley Service & Co.,Ltd, London, 1929: Chapter 6, Fig 3

Huangchao liqi tushi (reprint): Chapter 4, Fig 1

Library of Congress, Washington: Chapter 7, Fig 3

Palace Museum, Beijing: Chapter 1, Plate 1,2; Chapter 4, Fig 4; Chapter 8, Plate 1, 7

Royal Asiatic Society of Great Britain and Northern Ireland: Chapter 1, Fig 1

Urban Council Hong Kong from the collection of Hong Kong Museum of Art: Chapter 4, Plate 18; Chapter 6, Plate 10

Warner, John, *Fragrant Harbour,* John Warner Publications, Hong Kong, 1976: Chapter 7, Fig 6

Williams, C.A.S., *Outlines of Chinese Symbolism and Art Motives*, Customs College Press, Peking, 1931: Chapter 2, Fig 1

Woidt, H., *Chinese Handicrafts,* Peking, 1944: Chapter 5, Fig 3

Index

A Collector's Guide to
Chinese Dress Accessories

Designed by Tuck Loong
Edited by Elizabeth Berg

Published by Times Editions
an imprint of Times Editions Pte Ltd
Times Centre
1 New Industrial Road
Singapore 536196
Fax: (65)2854871 Tel: (65)2848844
e-mail: te@corp.tpl.com.sg

Printed in Malaysia by Times Offset Malaysia
ISBN: 981 204 729 8